EXTRAORDINARY

ORDINARY PEOPLE. EXTRAORDINARY GOD.

Darrin Patrick

LifeWay Press©
Nashville, TN

D1385202

ISBN: 978-1-4300-5978-3
Item number: 006104394

Dewey Decimal Classification Number: 248.83
Subject Heading: CHARACTER STUDY \ STUDENTS \ OLD TESTAMENT

Printed in the United States of America

Student Ministry Publishing
LifeWay Resources
One LifeWay Plaza
Nashville, TN 37234-0144

We believe that the Bible has God for its author; salvation for its end;
and truth, without any mixture of error, for its matter
and that all Scripture is totally true and trustworthy.
To review LifeWay's doctrinal guideline,
please visit *www.lifeway.com/doctrinalguideline.*

Contents

DARRIN PATRICK founded The Journey in 2002 in the urban core of St. Louis, Missouri. The Journey has six locations and has released seven church plants. Darrin is Vice President of the Acts 29 Church Planting Network and has helped start multiple non-profits in St. Louis. He also serves as Chaplain to the St. Louis Cardinals.

After earning his B.A. in Biblical languages from Southwest Baptist University and a Master's of Divinity from Midwestern Baptist Theological Seminary, Darrin earned his Doctor of Ministry from Covenant Seminary. Darrin is author of *The Dude's Guide to Manhood, Church Planter,* co-author of *Replant and For the City,* and contributor to the *ESV Gospel Transformation Bible* and *Don't Call it a Comeback.* He and his wife, Amie, recently released their first book, titled *The Dude's Guide to Marriage.*

Darrin and Amie have four beautiful children: Glory, Grace, Drew, and Delainey.

YOU CAN FIND MORE FROM DARRIN AND FOLLOW HIM AT:
> Blog/Resources: *DarrinPatrick.org*
> Twitter: *@DarrinPatrick*
> *Facebook.com/DarrinPatrick*
> *Instagram.com/drdarrinpatrick*
> *TheDudesGuide.org*

INTRO

If we're honest, many of us have drifted to a place of boredom or even doubt spiritually. Our lives seem limited and ordinary. Not only do we recognize that we're not perfect, sometimes we're painfully aware of past or current struggles. But deep down we have a longing for something more, something extraordinary.

The real question in all of our hearts, whether we know it or not, is:

CAN GOD USE ME?

The good news is that God is not asking us to be extraordinary. He's asking us to point to the One who is extraordinary—Jesus. In Scripture we see that God is in the business of taking flawed men and women and doing things through them that they never could have imagined.

Over the next six sessions, we'll look at the lives of:

> **ADAM** who was tempted to be extraordinary without God.

> **ABRAHAM** who responded to God's call to leave an extraordinary legacy.

> **MOSES** who experienced extraordinary power yet wrestled with self-doubt.

> **JOSHUA** who was given the extraordinary responsibility of leadership.

> **JOB** who trusted God without ever understanding his extraordinary suffering.

> **ESTHER** who reveals God's extraordinary sovereignty in ordinary decisions.

My prayer is that we'll clearly see that we're not supposed to be like these people. They were ordinary. God is extraordinary. We'll see that God invites us in our normal everyday lives to leave our boredom and negativity aside to join His extraordinary mission.

HOW TO USE

This Bible study includes six sessions of content. Every session has an introductory page summarizing the focus of study, followed by content designed for groups and for individuals.

GROUP SESSIONS

Regardless of what day or when your group meets, each session's content begins with the group session. This group session is designed to be one hour or more—with approximately 15 minutes of the time being teaching and 45 minutes being personal interaction. Of course, it's even better if your group is able to meet longer than an hour, allowing more time for your students connect with one another.

Each group session uses the following format to facilitate simple yet meaningful interaction among group members, with God's Word, and with the video teaching by Darrin Patrick.

Start

This page includes questions to get the conversation started, to review the previous session's practical application, and to introduce the video segment.

Watch

This page includes key points from Darrin Patrick's teaching, along with space for taking notes as participants watch the video.

Discuss

These two pages include questions and statements that guide the group to respond to the video teaching and to relevant Bible passages.

Pray

This final page of each group session includes a prompt for your closing time of prayer together and space for recording prayer requests of group members.

Leader Resources

For tips for leading a group, check out the leader resources on page 122.

INDIVIDUAL DISCOVERY

Each session includes options for students to study God's Word between sessions.

Moving Further

Following the group session prayer page is a weekly plan for students to engage with that session's focal point. No matter where students are in their walk with Christ, each session gives them the opportunity to study God's Word more deeply between sessions.

Students can choose to take advantage of some or all of the options provided. Those options are divided into the three categories of Worship, Personal Study, and Application.

Read

A seven-day reading plan is outlined for Scripture related to the group session and space for personal notes using the H.E.A.R. journaling method is provided.

Reflect

A one-page devotional option is provided each week to help students reflect on a biblical truth related to the group session.

Personal Study

Two personal study options are provided for each session. These pages are meant to take students deeper into Scripture, supplementing the biblical truths introduced in the teaching time. They will also challenge students to grow in their understanding of God's Word and to identify practical application in their own lives.

H.E.A.R. JOURNALING METHOD

Daily Bible Reading

Making time in you daily life to focus on God through His Word is a vital part of the Christian life. Even if you're unable to do anything else provided in this study during a certain session, try to spend time in God's Word. The verse selections will take you deeper into stories and truth related to the teaching and discussion during that group session.

Why Do You Need a Plan?

As a new believer or at other times in your life, you may find yourself in a place where you don't know where to begin reading your Bible, or how to personally approach Scripture. You may have tried the open-and-point method where you simply open your Bible and point to a verse, hoping to get something out of the random selection from God's Word. Reading random Scripture passages won't provide solid biblical growth any more then occasionally running around the block provides you with solid training to be an Olympic runner.

An effective plan must be well-balanced and consistent. When it comes to reading the Bible, well-balanced and consistent means reading and applying. A regular habit is great, but it's not enough to simply check a box off your task list when you've completed your daily reading. Knowing more about God is also great, but it's still not enough to read simply for spiritual knowledge. You have to respond to what you are reading by taking action as you listen to what God is saying. After all, it is God's Word.

It may seem intimidating or nerve-racking to study God's Word and journal about it, but we want to encourage you to use an extremely simple version of journaling called the H.E.A.R. method. (If this method helps you, also check out Robby and Kandi Gallaty's *Foundations: A 260-Day Bible Reading Plan for Busy Believers.*)

Journaling What You H.E.A.R. in God's Word

The H.E.A.R. journaling method promotes reading the Bible with a life-transforming purpose. Don't focus on checking off the boxes on your reading schedule. Your purpose is to read in order to understand and respond to God's Word in your life.

The H.E.A.R. acronym stands for Highlight, Explain, Apply, and Respond. Each of these four steps contributes to creating an atmosphere to hear God speak. After settling on a reading plan (like the one provided in this book for each session), decide on a time to study God's Word each day. Then you will be ready to hear from God.

Using the H.E.A.R. method means that whether you use a paper journal or your cell phone, you can record your H.E.A.R. journal anywhere.

Before You Begin—The Most Important Step

To really hear God speak to you through His Word, you always need to begin by praying. Pause and sincerely ask God to speak to you. It's absolutely necessary that we seek God's guidance in order to understand His Word (1 Cor. 2:12-14). Every time you read God's Word, simply pray like David prayed: "Open my eyes so that I may behold wondrous things out of your law" (Ps. 119:18).

H = HIGHLIGHT

After praying for the Holy Spirit's guidance, turn to the daily reading plan, and open your notes app on your phone, or use a journal if you'd like more space than provided in this book. For example, if you're reading Philippians 4:10-13, verse 13 may really jump out and speak to you as something you want to remember. You'd simply highlight, underline, or copy and paste Philippians 4:13.

At the top of the entry, write the Scripture reference, date, and a short title that summarizes the meaning of the passage.

E = EXPLAIN

After you've highlighted your verse(s), then explain what it means. Think about how you would summarize the passage in your own words. By asking some simple questions and with the help of God's Spirit, you can understand the meaning of the passage or verse. (A good study Bible can help you with answers to more in-depth questions as you learn to explain a passage of Scripture.) Try these questions to start:

> Why was it written?

> Who was the author, and who were they speaking to?

> How does the passage fit in with the verses before and after it?

> Why would the Holy Spirit include this passage in the book?

> What is God communicating through the text?

Next, below the "H," write the letter "E" and explain the passage in your own words. Record any answers to questions that help you understand the passage of Scripture.

A = APPLY

At this point, you are beginning the process of discovering the specific and personal message that God has for you from His Word. What is important is that you are engaging the text and wrestling with the meaning. Application is at the heart of growing closer to God. Asking yourself the following questions to begin uncovering how these verses will impact you personally:

> How can this help me?

> What is God saying to me?

> What would it look like to apply this verse in my life?

Next, write the letter "A" under the letter "E" where you wrote a short summary explaining the text. Challenge yourself to write several sentences about how the text applies to your life.

R = RESPOND

Finally, respond to the text. A personal response can take on many forms. You may write an action step to complete, describe a change in perspective, or simply respond in prayer to what you've learned. For example, you may ask for help being bold, need to repent of unconfessed sin, or you may simply need to praise God. Keep in mind that this is a response to what you have just read.

All of the words in the H.E.A.R. method are action words: Highlight, Explain, Apply, and Respond. God doesn't want us to sit back and wait for Him to drop truth into our laps. Instead of waiting passively, God desires that we actively pursue Him. Jesus said, "Ask, and it will be given to you; seek, and you will find; knock, and it will be opened to you" (Matt. 7:7).

Check out the example of the H.E.A.R. Journaling Method for reading Scripture on the next page, as well as My Group Covenant on page 13.

DATE: March 12, 2016

TITLE: Secret of Contentment

READING: Philippians 4:10-13

H (Highlight)

"I can do all things through him who strengthens me."
Philippians 4:13

E (Explain)

Paul was telling the church at Philippi that he had discovered the secret of contentment. No matter the situations in Paul's life, he realized that Christ was all he needed, and Christ was the One who strengthened him to persevere through difficult times.

A (Apply)

In my life, I will experience many ups and downs. My contentment is not found in circumstances. Rather, it is based on my relationship with Jesus Christ. Only Jesus gives me the strength I need to be content in every circumstance of life.

R (Respond)

Lord Jesus, please help me as I strive to be content in You. Remind me that it is only by Your strength that I can make it through any situation I must face.

MY GROUP COVENANT

As I begin *Extraordinary* with my small group, I acknowledge authentic Christian community requires commitment to participate with others and invest myself during and even beyond each session. As I begin this journey with my small group, I commit to:

> Study God's Word each day.

> Complete the Personal Study sections between sessions.

> Come prepared and ready to discuss God's Word with the group.

> Respect the opinions and discussions of others.

> Spend time in prayer for those in the group with me each week.

> Encourage and connect with my group between sessions.

_____

Signature

_____

Date

ADAM

SESSION 1

Adam and Eve were placed into a world that was perfectly designed for them to connect with God. This first man and woman were unique among all of creation as God's image-bearers (Gen. 1:26-27). Walking in the garden in the cool of the day, they experienced an extraordinary relationship with God. They were called to rule over God's creation in His name and for His glory.

As they honored God as Creator and their ultimate authority, they were free to enjoy His creation. But everything changed after being offered a taste of life apart from God. Satan tempted Adam and Eve with the opportunity to be "like God" (Gen. 3:5). Though they were already created in God's "likeness" (Gen. 1:26), they gave into forbidden fruit and tasted death. Life as they knew it spiraled downward into what we call the fall of man.

They believed lies about God and themselves.

Sin entered the world.

Shame entered their hearts.

They hid.

Now, we all do the same.

So, the Creator entered His creation. Our only hope is in Jesus—God become man—who tasted death for us so that we may experience life through faith. The Word of God offers us the wisdom we now need to overcome temptation and walk in freedom by the power of the Holy Spirit.

START

Welcome students to the first group session.

Spend a few minutes getting to know and hanging out with one another.

Use the following to start your time together.

In the last few years, superheroes have made a dramatic comeback onto the big screen. Marvel seems to put out a summer blockbuster each year. Even biblical stories have been turned into heroic adventures—using creative license—with Darren Aronofsky's *Noah* and Ridley Scott's *Exodus: God and Kings*.

> **What is it about heroes and epic stories that captures our imagination?**

Stories like these invite us to imagine the extraordinary. Deep down, we want to be extraordinary ourselves, not just witness it around us. We don't want to just behold the heroic, we want to be heroic.

In the next six sessions, we want to unearth that buried desire for more. We want to learn how each of us can be used by God to do extraordinary things. In each session we'll spotlight a so-called hero in the Old Testament to see how they were truly ordinary people with an extraordinary and powerful God.

Let's see what Darrin has to say about God's original plan for mankind at the beginning of the story, right there in the first few pages of the Bible.

Pray for God to speak to your students' hearts and minds before showing the video for Session 1.

WATCH

- -

Use the space below to follow along and take notes as you watch the video for Session 1.

1. Paradise wasn't paradise without _____.

2. Paradise wasn't paradise without _____.

3. We have a desire to bring _____ out of _____.

4. Any time a person doesn't follow the _____ of God, it's because they're following a _____ of Satan.

5. Satan tempts us with the offer of becoming _____ apart from God.

6. Though we fail to _____ to God in our sin, God _____ to us in our sin.

Scripture: Genesis 1-3

1. relationship 2. work 3. order, chaos 4. truth, lie 5. extraordinary 6. go, comes

DISCUSS

- -

Use the statements and questions below to discuss the video.

Darrin explained that we were created for extraordinary relationship with God and given extraordinary responsibility from God.

> **How does this affect your view of God, yourself, or others?**

Being made "in the image of God" means that we have been designed to reflect God's character in this world.

> **What comes to mind when you think of God's character?**

> **What is most meaningful to you about God's character?**

> **Which parts of God's character are hardest for you to reflect? Why?**

Darrin identified our work as one way we reflect God's image. He defines work (*management*) as bringing order out of chaos.

> **Where do you see chaos in the world or in your own life?**

> **How can you seek to bring order out of chaos in your own life and in the world?**

> **How does knowing that God made you a steward (*overseer*) of His creation transform the way you approach relationships and responsibilities?**

In Genesis 3, we see chaos enter our lives as relationships and responsibilities are neglected. Let's look at the words of the serpent (*Satan*):

Read aloud Genesis 3:1-6.

> **How did the serpent tempt Eve?**

> **What can you learn from Adam and Eve's disregard toward sin?**

> **Temptation is always a lie. What are some specific examples of how temptation promises something extraordinary apart from God?**

Read aloud Genesis 3:7-13.

> ### What does this passage reveal about God and the consequences of sin?

In a tragic and almost laughable event, Adam and Eve try hiding from God. Then Adam has the audacity to blame Eve (and God for making Eve) for his sin. Eve, in turn, blames the serpent for her sin.

> ### What are some things we use to try to hide from God and cover our own sin?

> ### What excuses do we make for our sin?

Adam not only failed to obey God, but he also failed to protect his wife. Theologians distinguish between sins of commission and sins of omission. As Darrin said it, we can fail by being "intentionally aggressive" or "intentionally passive."

> ### What's an example of a sin of omission?

> ### With which of your relationships or responsibilities do you struggle with passivity?

> ### How can you be more alert and proactive in those relationships?

The consequences of Adam and Eve's sin were real and lasting. But the good news is that their story didn't end behind trees and fig leaves. Even though they hid from God, He came to them. He even provided for them.

Read aloud Genesis 3:9 and 21.

> ### Describe a way God has pursued you in a place or time when you weren't looking for Him.

> ### What evidence of God's provision and grace do you see in your life?

> ### What else has been challenging, encouraging, or insightful from today's study of Adam?

Conclude your group time with the prayer activity on the following page. Complete the personal study for Session 1 before the next session.

PRAY

We all carry on Adam's legacy of passivity. Satan, our tempter and accuser, wants it that way. He wants us to give into temptation, seeking to be extraordinary on our own, turning away from God and other people. His primary weapons are lies to make us doubt God's goodness.

Spend a few minutes as a group naming lies that Satan speaks to us.

Share a lie that is constantly whispered in your ear by the Enemy.

Read aloud the following passage from Peter's first letter. Close by praying for vigilance against the deadly lies of our Enemy and come to God with humble faith in His goodness.

> 6 Humble yourselves, therefore, under the mighty hand of God so that at the proper time he may exalt you, 7 casting all your anxieties on him, because he cares for us. 8 Be sober-minded; be watchful. Your adversary the devil prowls around like a roaring lion, seeking someone to devour.
> **1 Peter 5:6-8**

PRAYER REQUESTS

MOVING FURTHER

In addition to studying God's Word, work with your group leader to create a personal plan for worship, personal study, and application between now and the next session. Select from the following optional activities to match your personal preferences and available time.

WORSHIP

> Read your Bible. Complete the reading plan on page 22.

> Spend time with God by engaging the devotional on page 23.

> Connect with God each day through prayer.

PERSONAL STUDY

> Read and interact with "The Process of Temptation" on page 24.

> Read and interact with "Overcoming Temptation" on page 28.

APPLICATION

> Identify some area of your life (home, school, team, etc.) where there is "chaos." Consider how you might bring some order to that situation.

> Memorize 1 Corinthians 10:13: "No temptation has overtaken you that is not common to man. God is faithful, and he will not let you be tempted beyond your ability, but with the temptation he will also provide the way of escape, that you may be able to endure it."

> Find another Christ follower you might consider meeting with each week to ask questions about the temptations you face and to pray for one another.

> Start a journal to record the times that you see where God has pursued you even when you've hidden from Him due to sin. Use this as a way to remind yourself of God's love and forgiveness when you feel the shame of sin.

READ

Read through the following Scripture passages this week. Use the acronym H.E.A.R. and the space provided to record your thoughts or action steps.

Day 1: Genesis 1

Day 2: Genesis 2

Day 3: Genesis 3:1-13

Day 4: Genesis 3:14-24

Day 5: Romans 5:12-21

Day 6: Romans 6:1-14

Day 7: 1 Corinthians 15:12-28

REFLECT

TREE OF THE KNOWLEDGE OF GOOD AND EVIL

It's common for us to envision Adam and Eve walking around their lush garden and gazing upon this beautiful fruit tree, which they can't "enjoy," right in the middle of it all. With this picture in mind, it's easy to wonder: *Did God set Adam and Eve up to fail? We know Satan tempted them, but did God make it easier?*

Let's look closer at how the Bible describes Eden, specifically the trees:

> "And out of the ground the LORD God made to spring up every tree that is pleasant to the sight and good for food."
> **Genesis 2:9**

> "So when the woman saw that the tree was good for food, and that it was a delight to the eyes...she took of its fruit and ate..."
> **Genesis 3:6**

Notice there were more than a just a few trees in the garden. Also, notice the description of the tree of the knowledge of good and evil is essentially the same as all the other trees in the garden, which they could enjoy. It wasn't any more pleasing or fruitful!

The way Satan tempted Adam and Eve was to have them forget about all the other trees. He wanted them to believe that God was withholding something good from them, that God was being stingy. The way we fight against temptation is by paying attention to all the other "trees" God has provided.

List ways God has blessed you with "pleasant" things to enjoy.

PERSONAL STUDY 1

THE PROCESS OF TEMPTATION

The Book of James in the New Testament provides us with one of the clearest descriptions of how temptation works. In addition to discussing the Devil, our most obvious Enemy, James identifies two other enemies we all have.

> [1] What causes quarrels and what causes fights among you? Is it not this, that your passions, are at war within you? [2] You desire and do not have, so you murder. You covet and cannot obtain, so you fight and quarrel. You do not have because you do not ask. [3] You ask and do not receive, because you ask wrongly, to spend it on your passions. [4] You adulterous people! Do you not know that friendship with the world is enmity with God? Therefore whoever wishes to be a friend of the world makes himself an enemy of God. [5] Or do you suppose that the Scripture says, "He yearns jealously over the spirit that he has made to dwell in us"? [6] But he gives more grace. Therefore it says, "God opposes the proud, but gives grace to the humble." [7] Submit yourselves therefore to God. Resist the devil, and he will flee from you. [8] Draw near to God, and he will draw near to you. Cleanse your hands, you sinners, and purify your hearts, you double-minded.
> **James 4:1-8**

Our three enemies are the flesh, the world, and the Devil.

1. The flesh is that part of us not yet submitted to God.

2. The world is the corporate expression of the flesh—many people living as if God does not exist.

3. The Devil is a fallen angel who opposes God and His people.

How does each one of our enemies play upon our passions?

Of these three enemies, which one does James speak about the most in the passage you read?

What does the emphasis on that Enemy tell you about the nature of temptation?

A key to fighting temptation is to recognize that many sins are not merely single acts, but are the result of an unchecked process. Look at how James describes the process:

> [12] Blessed is the man who remains steadfast under trial, for when he has stood the test of time he will receive the crown of life, which God has promised to those who love him. [13] Let no one say when he is tempted, "I am being tempted by God," for God cannot be tempted with evil, and he himself tempts no one. [14] But each person is tempted when he is lured and enticed by his own desire. [15] Then desire when it has conceived gives birth to sin, and sin when it is fully grown brings forth death.
> **James 1:12-15**

James uses two metaphors to describe the process of temptation.

The first (in v. 14) is a fishing metaphor. Even if you've never been fishing yourself, you know the basic principle: you've got to hide the hook. You need bait. The reason sin looks good to us is because we are only seeing the bait. We are like fish biting down on the hook. We focus on the short-term pleasure (*the bait*), and fail to see the long-term consequences (*the hook*).

Consider a current temptation you are experiencing.

What is the bait?

What is the hook?

The second metaphor (in v. 15) uses human growth. It may be easier to understand it by looking at a tree and how it progresses from a seed that's been planted to a full grown tree. All sinful actions begin as a seed in the human heart—a small desire that begins to grow. Our whole beings are involved in this process. Our emotions latch onto something. *I want that. I have to have that.* Our mind rationalizes and justifies it. *It's not that bad. No one will see.* Then our will acts upon it. That tiny desire becomes an action that results in a consequence. The seemingly harmless baby steps, a little thing here and there, eventually lead us down a path into full-grown sinfulness that we never would've imagined. In the end, sin is always destructive.

So, for each sin, ask the following questions: What is the seed (*desire*)? What is the sapling (*action step*)? What is the tree (*consequence*)?

Take lust for example. What is the seed? *You are attracted to someone.* What is the sapling? *You begin to fantasize about them.* What is the tree? *You have sex outside of the marriage covenant.*

How would this growth process play out with anger?

Seed:

Sapling:

Tree:

Consider another temptation you have dealt with. Identify the growth process from desire, to action, to consequence.

Seed:

Sapling:

Tree:

The wisdom that James provides is crucial in understanding how temptation works. Even starting to identify this process in our own lives is an important tool for resisting temptation. In our next study, we'll look at how we can overcome temptation.

Close your study time in prayer, asking God for awareness of temptation and the strength to resist.

PERSONAL STUDY 2

OVERCOMING TEMPTATION

Even though we have enemies from outside (Satan and the world) and from within (the flesh), it's possible to resist temptation. Read these words from the apostle Paul:

> No temptation has overtaken you that is not common to man. God is faithful, and he will not let you be tempted beyond your ability, but with the temptation he will also provide the way of escape, that you may be able to endure it.
> **1 Corinthians 10:13**

How does Paul challenge you in this passage?

What hope does Paul give in this passage?

One of the reasons we give into temptation is because we try to face it alone. We are prone to hide from God and one another—just like Adam and Eve.

When have you tried to overcome a recurring sin on your own, and how successful were you?

What fear(s) prevented you from confessing that struggle to another Christ follower?

Paul reminds us that we are not alone. Other people have experienced temptations like ours. Other people can identify with our struggles. So, we can turn to others for help. God Himself can identify with our struggle. Notice what the Book of Hebrews says about Jesus and temptation.

> Therefore he had to be made like his brothers in every respect, so that he might become a merciful and faithful high priest in the service of God, to make propitiation for the sins of the people. For because he himself has suffered when tempted, he is able to help those who are being tempted.
>
> **Hebrews 2:17-18**

How does it encourage you to know that Jesus can relate to you in the temptations you face?

What would it look like practically for Jesus to help you resist temptation in your life?

One way, if not the most significant one, is through prayer—both Jesus' and ours. In what we often refer to as "The High Priestly Prayer" (John 17), we see how Jesus prayed to the Father, specifically asking for protection for His original disciples and future disciples, saying: "I do not ask that you take them out of the world, but that you keep them from the evil one" (John 17:15). Now seated at the right hand of the Father, "he always lives to make intercession" for "those who draw near to God through him" (Heb. 7:25).

Jesus also receives our prayers. Believers are encouraged to "draw near to the throne of grace, that we may receive mercy and find grace to help in time of need" (Heb. 4:16). We come near "with confidence" (4:16) because Jesus is able "to sympathize with our weaknesses" since He was "in every respect tempted as we are" (4:15). Jesus understands our struggles. His ears are open to us.

How does the truth that Jesus is our High Priest affect the way you pray?

Now, the Gospels actually record Jesus' first encounter with Satan (Matt. 4:1-11; Mark 1:12-13; Luke 4:1-13). After His baptism, Jesus was led into the wilderness to be tempted (*tested*) in preparation for His public ministry.

Read Matthew 4:1-11.

With what three things does Satan tempt Jesus?

How does Jesus respond each time?

How should this shape the way you should respond to temptation?

While we can look to Jesus as an example in our fight against temptation, we need more than someone to sympathize with us in our weakness. We need someone to save us from our sin. That is why it is of the highest importance that Jesus faced temptation "without sin" (Heb. 4:15). His sinless life was a necessary requirement in becoming the perfect sacrifice on the cross. He not only resisted Satan, but He also defeated him:

> 14 Since therefore the children share in flesh and blood, he himself likewise partook of the same things, that through death he might destroy the one who has the power of death, that is, the devil, 15 and deliver all those who through fear of death were subject to lifelong slavery.
>
> **Hebrews 2:14-15**

On the cross, Jesus "bruised" Satan's "head," but Satan only "bruised his heel" (Gen. 3:15). Where the first Adam was tempted by Satan and failed, Jesus, the "last Adam" (1 Cor. 15:45), was tempted by Satan and succeeded. Now, we share in His victory.

Close your study time in prayer, thanking God for victory over sin and death.

ABRAHAM

SESSION 2

Abraham was an old man when God called him to leave everything he had ever worked for behind in exchange for an even greater legacy. Following God meant leaving his home and most of his family. Following God meant leaving what was comfortable for what was unknown.

All he had to rely on in making this decision was God's promise. He would bless Abraham, making him a great nation and a great name. This was an extraordinary promise, especially for a man whose wife was unable to have children.

But the blessing was not for Abraham alone. Through his offspring, God was going to bless "all the families of the earth" (Gen. 12:3).

Thousands of years later, we're now a part of that blessing and calling. God calls us to join in His redemptive mission. It brings Him great glory to work primarily through broken, sinful people, rather than work around them.

Responding to God's call always means leaving something precious, but it's always in pursuit of the greater legacy that God wants us to take part in.

START

Welcome students back to the second group session.

Use the following to start your time together.

At the end of Session 1, we looked for areas where we are prone to passivity and vulnerable to the lies of our Enemy.

What areas of passivity in your life have you recognized that you would be comfortable sharing with the group?

What did you learn about temptation as you completed your personal study in Session 1?

How can you be sensitive to God's presence and pursuit of you after the last session?

In Session 1, we saw that God designed us for an intimate relationship with Him and assigned us the great responsibility of stewarding His creation. But chaos entered the world through man's sin.

In the video for this session, Darrin explores the life of Abraham, one of the most well-known biblical figures, second only to Jesus. We'll see how God continues to pursue a relationship with His people, by calling Abraham to leave a life of comfort and security for the sake of a greater mission and legacy.

Pray for God to open each student's heart and mind before showing the video for Session 2.

WATCH

- -

Use the space below to follow along and take notes as you watch the video for Session 2.

1. If you want to understand a man, look at his _____, his _____, and his _____.*

2. Responding to God's call always means _____ something precious.

3. A change in name means a change in _____ and a change in _____.

4. God blesses us so we can be a _____.

Scriptures: Genesis 12, 13, 15, 17, 22

***Leader Note:** *Guide students to consider that they can understand others by evaluating the relationships around them. Even though students won't be able to relate specifically to having a husband or wife, they will have other adults in their lives who are married that they can look to and ask about relationships.*

1. dad, wife, pain 2. leaving 3. character, agenda 4. blessing

DISCUSS

Use the following statements and questions to discuss the video.

No matter how history looks back on Abraham, Darrin explained that he started as an ordinary guy before God called him. In what ways can you can relate to Abraham?

There are three ways we often avoid God's call on our lives:

1. **Ignore** — Pretend God didn't say it

2. **Question** — Act like you don't know what it means

3. **Negotiate** — Argue with God about what He is asking you to do

When you sense God calling you to do something, which of these three avoidance responses comes most naturally for you?

How do we sometimes try to avoid what God is calling us to do in our lives?

Read aloud Genesis 12:1-9.

What does this passage reveal about God and Abraham?

Darrin said that responding to God's call means leaving something precious.

What are some of the more challenging things you've had to leave behind to follow God?

Darrin observed that in order to follow God, Abraham had to become a nomad, like the people he likely felt superior to for most of his life.

When has God's call in your life revealed pride in your heart?

Abraham also had to step into uncertainty. God was leading him to a new land, but he had not shown him that land yet. Hebrews 11:8 echoes Genesis 12:1: "And he went out, not knowing where he was going." He had to act before he knew all the details.

When was the last time that following God meant walking into uncertainty for you?

When you sense God's calling for you to act without knowing all the details, how do you find the faith to obey?

Re-read God's call to Abraham in Genesis 12:1-3.

Ultimately, what led Abraham to leave comfort and step into uncertainty was God's promise of a greater legacy. But though God's call was for Abraham, it wasn't just about Abraham. There was a larger purpose. God blessed Abraham so that he would be a blessing.

How have you seen believers use their positions or resources to bless the people and families in their communities?

What are some tangible blessings that God has given to you?

What would it look like for you to be a blessing to your teachers, family, team, or classmates?

How has this session challenged or encouraged you in your relationship with Christ?

Conclude this session with your students by using the prayer activity on the following page. Complete the personal study for Session 2 before the next session.

PRAY

Take time to try to identify one thing (even if it seems insignificant) that you sense God is calling you to leave in order to follow Him in a new way. This could mean walking away from an activity at school, playing fewer video games, or even the way you use social media. Write your answers to the three questions below in the space provided. After a few minutes, gather in smaller groups of two or three to share.

What is God calling me to leave?

What is uncertain about the result?

How might this serve to bless others?

Pray together that the answer to the final question would help you overcome any impulse to ignore, question, or negotiate with God.

PRAYER REQUESTS

MOVING FURTHER

In addition to studying God's Word, work with your group leader to create a plan for worship, personal study, and application between now and the next session. Select from the following optional activities to match your personal preferences and available time.

WORSHIP

› Read your Bible. Complete the reading plan on page 40.

› Spend time with God by engaging the devotion on page 41.

› Connect with God each day through prayer.

PERSONAL STUDY

› Read and interact with "Discovering God's Call" on page 42.

› Read and interact with "Not Once, But Twice" on page 46.

APPLICATION

› Memorize Genesis 12:2: "And I will make of you a great nation and I will bless you and make your name great, so that you will be a blessing."

› Connect with someone from your group this week. Set aside time to meet somewhere at your school, a coffee shop, or a friend's house. When you meet, ask each other two questions: (1) Is there anything God is calling you to leave in order to follow Him? (2) How can I help you in that? Then plan to follow-up in the coming weeks.

› To continue using your journal, write down the different things that you have had to leave behind in order to follow Jesus. Also list ways in which God has provided for you.

READD

Read through the following Scripture passages this week. Use the space provided to record your thoughts and responses.

Day 1: Genesis 12:1-9

Day 2: Genesis 12:10-20

Day 3: Genesis 15:1-19

Day 4: Genesis 16:1-15

Day 5: Genesis 17:1-14

Day 6: Genesis 21:1-21

Day 7: Genesis 22

REFLECT

WAITING PATIENTLY

Though Abraham is commended for his faith in the New Testament (see Heb. 11), his faith was by no means consistent. He was often impatient about his circumstances. Unwilling to wait for God, he tried to take matters into his own hands and it backfired.

Not once, but twice, he lied and put his wife, Sarah, in danger because he did not trust God's protection (Gen. 12:10-20; 20:1-18). Even more devastating, Abraham doubted God's promise that Sarah would bear children, and he conceived a child, Ishmael, through a female servant, Hagar (Gen. 16). His failure to trust God led to greater pain and dysfunction in his life (and in the lives of others).

It's important to remember that our sin (even impatience when waiting on God's timing) doesn't only affect us. We saw this in Session 1 with Adam, now with Abraham, and we will see it next week with Moses. It's a pattern of sin that's a struggle for each of us.

There are few commands in Scripture more difficult than waiting on God, but often they are connected to God's faithful provision. On his own, Abraham would have utterly ruined himself and his family. But God was patient with Abraham.

God was faithful to deliver on His promises. We all find ourselves in times of waiting, hoping that our current circumstances will change. As you ask God for the patience to trust in His timing, reflect on this truth from Scripture:

> 25 The LORD is good to those who wait for Him, to the soul who seeks him.
> **Lamentations 3:25**

PERSONAL STUDY 1

DISCOVERING GOD'S CALL

Even if you related to Abraham in certain ways after watching and discussing the video, you may still be struggling with what God's call really means. When God spoke to Abraham, it was so clear and direct. Why doesn't it always feel that way for us?

In an important sense, Abraham's call was unique. He had a specific role within God's overall redemptive plan. But that doesn't mean we can't learn from Abraham's call. In fact, if we look more closely at what the Bible tells us about Abraham's call, we may find more encouragement there than we would at first glance.

First, notice that the Bible tells us that Abraham received his call from God in two different locations. According to Genesis 11:31-32, God called Abraham in Haran. But when Stephen (the first Christian martyr) tells Abraham's story to the religious leaders of his day, he says that God called Abraham in Ur, "the land of the Chaldeans" before he lived in Haran (Acts 7:2).

So, which one is it? While some skeptics may choose to believe that the New Testament or Stephen himself got it wrong, the answer is both. It's very likely that God began to call Abraham while he was in Ur, and then when his father moved the family to Haran, God revealed even more to Abraham at that point. As we'll see next session, sometimes God just grabs people's attention immediately, but often he does it step by step.

> **How has figuring out God's call in your life been a step by step process?**

Not only can God's call vary in timing, it can vary in method. When we read about the apostle Paul's missionary journeys in the Book of Acts, we know that the Holy Spirit guided him. Apart from direct revelation by the Holy Spirit, there were at least three different forms that guidance took.

1. **God's clear priorities.** The Book of Acts opens with Jesus telling His disciples that they will be his witnesses in Jerusalem, Judea, Samaria and to the ends of the earth (Acts 1:8). The Gospel of Matthew ends with the Great Commission, where Jesus commands his disciples to go and make more disciples. The clear priority given to Paul was to preach the gospel to the Gentiles. He didn't always know where and how that would take place. But it influenced every decision he made.

What are some of the clear priorities that influence your decisions?

On a scale of 0-10 (0 = *not at all* and 10 = *perfectly*) how well do your priorities align with God's priorities you see in Scripture? Circle your answer.

0   1   2   3   4   5   6   7   8   9   10

What caused you to rate your priorities the way you did?

What would help you better align your priorities with God's?

2. **God's response to prayer.** While Paul was at the church in Antioch, the Holy Spirit said, "Set apart for me Barnabas and Saul for the work to which I have called them" (Acts 13:2b). But notice how that passage begins, "Now there were in the church at Antioch prophets and teachers," and "While they were worshiping the Lord and fasting, the Holy Spirit said..." (13:1-2a). It is clear that they were actively seeking God's will before the Holy Spirit provided clarity.

What does your prayer look like when you are trying to determine God's will?

Who do you normally talk to when you are trying to determine God's will?

3. **God's response to our action.** At times, our experience of this is more like trial and error. Consider how Luke describes one portion of Paul's journey, "And they went through the region of Phrygia and Galatia, having been forbidden by the Holy Spirit to speak the word in Asia. And when they had come up to Mysia, they attempted to go into Bithynia, but the Spirit of Jesus did not allow them. So, passing by Mysia, they went down to Troas" (Acts 16:6-8). While it is entirely possible that the Holy Spirit directly spoke to Paul and Timothy in those places, they may have just experienced insurmountable obstacles that were understood as the Spirit closing doors. Either way, they went one way. Door closed. Then they went another direction. Door closed. After multiple unsuccessful attempts, the Holy Spirit finally told them where to go.

Discerning and following God's call requires risk as you take real life steps to align your priorities with His. Think back to the prayer activity that concluded the last session. Let's include today's steps of determining God's will.

What things are you trying to determine about God's calling for your life?

What would it cost you to step out in faith and follow God's calling in your life?

What is risky or uncertain about it? Are you willing to take the risk? Why or why not?

What do you need to prioritize in order to be obedient?

How could your decision to take a step of faith influence and encourage others?

Pray that you would take action with your answer to the last question about taking a step of faith. Ask God to help you follow Him in obedience for the sake of His mission.

PERSONAL STUDY 2

NOT ONCE, BUT TWICE

In Hebrews 11, there is a list of people which is often called "the hall of fame of faith." Abraham is commended not once, but twice, for leaving something precious in order to follow God. We've already discussed the first "leaving":

> By faith Abraham obeyed when he was called to go out to a place that he was to receive as an inheritance. And he went out, not knowing where he was going. By faith he went to live in the land of promise, as in a foreign land, living in tents with Isaac and Jacob, heirs with him of the same promise.
> **Hebrews 11:8-9**

Just to give us another picture of the significance of God's call to Abraham, Old Testament professor Sandra Richter translates as we'd understand it today:

> Leave your house, your job, your friends, your church, your relatives, abandon your inheritance, a 401K that will not transfer and maybe even the equity in your home—and go somewhere you don't speak the language, you have no business contacts, friends, or relatives . . . and trust God to make a new place for you.[1]

But believe it or not, that may not have been as hard as the next he is commended for:

> By faith Abraham, when he was tested, offered up Isaac, and he who had received the promises was in the act of offering up his only son, of whom it was said, "Through Isaac shall your offspring be named."
> **Hebrews 11:17-18**

The first time Abraham encounters God is when he's asked to leave everything behind. There is no indication that he knew of God at all before that point. The only thing God could offer Abraham in his old age that he didn't already have was children. His wife, Sarah, was unable to have children (Gen. 11:30). God promising to "make him into a great nation" (12:2), implying offspring, was all that Abraham needed to hear. Still it was no small thing for him to trust God to even provide in that way!

When was the first time you experienced God's call on your life (i.e. through a parent, sibling, friend, youth leader, or pastor)?

If you've never felt a specific calling, describe a time when you realized what God desired for you to do as a Christian in general.

In all your questions and hesitations, was there one specific promise or hope that encouraged you to follow Him?

How long did you have to wait before you saw that promise fulfilled, that hope realized? Are you still waiting?

Already 75 years old, Abraham had to wait another 25 years before Isaac was born! Long before that point he and Sarah had lost not just patience, but trust that God would deliver on His promise. After listening to God's Word for 10 years, Sarah said to Abram:

> 2 "Behold now, the LORD has prevented me from bearing children. Go in to my servant; it may be that I shall obtain children by her." And Abram listened to the voice of Sarai.
> **Genesis 16:2**

It didn't help that Sarah immediately felt jealousy and anger toward Hagar when she conceived a son, Ishmael (despite it being her plan!). On top of that, he would not be the child of the promise. Despite the unbelief of Abraham and Sarah, and the dysfunction they introduced into their lives, God was gracious to Ishmael and blessed him, but He did not establish His covenant with him.

Displaying His extraordinary power within creation, God visited Sarah as He had promised, and she conceived and bore Isaac to Abraham when he was a hundred years old (21:1-7). After waiting a lifetime for their son, it must have felt like a blink of the eye before God sought to test Abraham. God told Abraham to sacrifice Isaac as a burnt offering (22:2).

What is your initial reaction to God's call in this passage?

How do you make sense of what may seem like an outrageous request?

Now, consider how the Bible addresses Abraham's motivation for obedience:

> He considered that God was able even to raise him from the dead, from which, figuratively speaking, he did receive him back.
> **Hebrews 11:19**

Abraham was willing to "leave" Isaac because he knew God would be faithful to His covenant promises. Abraham knew that Isaac was his "only son" (11:17) with regard to the covenant. God's faithfulness was bound to Isaac's existence. Abraham knew that God would somehow resolve it. He had faith that God would remain faithful to His covenant even when it seemed there was no earthly way it would be possible.

Based on this discussion of Abraham's faith, how would you define faith?

Read Hebrews 11:1. How does this verse compare with your definition of faith?

What does this verse add to your understanding of faith?

Pray now for faith that moves you to action, even when you cannot see what God is doing or understand how it will all work out.

MOSES

SESSION 3

Any time God puts a call on your life, you're going to have questions.

You may have some doubts or even a few excuses as to why God should find someone else for the job. Some of this will be natural, as God may ask you to do things that make no earthly sense at all.

That was the case for Moses.

God called him to lead his people out of slavery in Egypt. How was this fugitive shepherd with a speech problem supposed to stand up before Pharaoh and walk away alive—much less with all the Israelites following him?

And yet, God promised to be with Moses. When Moses finally overcame his reluctance, he found himself in the front row watching God rescue His people and provide for them in spectacular and supernatural ways.

At some point along the way, however, Moses grew weary—as we all do when we try to fulfill God's call in our own strength. Leading a stubborn and stiff-necked people with short-term memory, Moses gets frustrated and makes the biggest mistake of his life trying to exercise his own will above God's—one that would prevent him from entering the promised land.

START

Welcome students back to the third group session.

Use the following to start your time together.

In the previous group session, we were asked to consider something (no matter how small it may seem) that God is calling us to leave in order to follow Him.

> **As you spent time in God's Word and in prayer since the last session, did you sense God calling or reminding you to do something?**

> **What steps of faith did you take in response to God's call this week? If you did not take any, why not?**

> **From your personal study in Session 2, what were some of the key takeaways on waiting, God's guidance, and faith?**

In this session, we'll learn more about how God's call on our lives is for the sake of others. We'll explore the life of Moses, who wrestled with doubt even as he led the Israelites out of bondage in Egypt. Let's watch as Darrin connects Moses' story to our story.

Pray for God to open students' hearts and minds before showing the video for Session 3.

WATCH

- -

Use the space below to follow along and take notes as you watch the video for Session 3.

1. God is _____, but He's also _____.

2. Any time God puts a call on your life, you'll have _____.

3. Moses is tired, frustrated, and disconnected from God when he makes the biggest _____ of his life.

4. What happens to Moses is what happens to us. We try _____ accomplish _____ _____ in our own strength.

5. God will work in _____ and through _____, despite us.

Scriptures: Exodus 3:5-8;11-12, Isaiah 6:1-5, Numbers 20:2-13

1. holy, compassionate 2. questions 3. mistake 4. to, God's work 5. us, us

DISCUSS

Use the following statements and questions below to discuss the video.

Darrin picked up Moses' story from when God called him in the wilderness. But let's be reminded of why Moses was in the wilderness in the first place.

Read aloud Exodus 2:11-15.

As we see from this passage, Moses tried to do something about the pain he saw, but his violent response only added to the pain. So, he hid in the wilderness as a fugitive and tried to start over with a new family.

When have you tried to fix a broken situation, but only added to the brokenness?

How does that past experience affect how you engage broken situations now?

What does God's appearance in the wilderness reveal about God?

Why do you think God chose to meet Moses in the wilderness?

Darrin said that God's attention-getting devices are invitations for us to think about and behold His character. Specifically through the burning bush, God was revealing Himself as both holy and compassionate.

What are some things God has used to get your attention?

Even though God revealed Himself in such a dramatic way, Moses questioned whether he could really do what God was calling him to do.

Instruct a student to read Exodus 4:1-14 aloud.

Why do you think Moses doubted God even after seeing the signs He gave him?

Despite Moses' objections and reluctance, God still did extraordinary things through him. Here are a just a few: parting the Red Sea (Ex. 14), bringing water out of the rock (Ex. 17), delivering the Ten Commandments (Ex. 20). And throughout all of these God was with him. Consider how Exodus 33:11 describes the closeness of their relationship, "the LORD used to speak to Moses face to face, as a man speaks to his friend."

How does it encourage you to know that God blessed someone who was doubtful?

Moses was constantly frustrated by the grumbling and complaining of the people. Instead of resting in his relationship with God, he again tried to accomplish God's work in his own strength. As Darrin explained from Numbers 20, Moses vented his frustration in a sinful way, cursing the people and disobeying God's clear command.

How can you tell when you are trying to do God's work in your own strength?

What do you think is the real reason you attempt to act out of your own strength?

When are you likely to become frustrated and doubt? What does it look like to invite God into your frustration?

Where in Moses' story can you find confidence that God will treat you with compassion?

What else has been challenging, encouraging, or insightful from your study of Moses?

Conclude your group time with the prayer activity on the following page. Complete the personal study for Session 3 before the next session.

PRAY

Despite having such unique access to God, Moses often locked his eyes on his own limitations and his frustration with other people. Isn't that the case for all of us? This caused him to lose sight of promises from God like this one:

> "My presence will go with you, and I will give you rest."
> **Exodus 33:14**

We are prone to a similar struggle in the task before us as followers of Christ. Let's read aloud "The Great Commission" in Matthew 28:

> [16] Now the eleven disciples went to Galilee, to the mountain to which Jesus had directed them. [17] And when they saw him they worshiped him, but some doubted. [18] And Jesus came and said to them, "All authority in heaven and on earth has been given to me. [19] Go therefore and make disciples of all nations, baptizing them in the name of the Father and of the Son and of the Holy Spirit, [20] teaching them to observe all that I have commanded you. And behold, I am with you always, to the end of the age."
> **Matthew 28:16-20**

Write these two verses, or at least the Scripture references, on opposite sides of an index card or piece of paper, or make it your phone background to keep with you this week. Any time you feel doubtful or frustrated, look at these verses to remind yourself of God's promise of His power and presence to fulfill His calling.

Pray now for confidence in our extraordinary God who is always with us.

PRAYER REQUESTS

MOVING FURTHER

In addition to studying God's Word, work with your group leader to create a plan for worship, personal study, and application between now and the next session. Select from the following optional activities to match your personal preferences and available time.

WORSHIP

› Read your Bible. Complete the reading plan on page 58.

› Spend time with God by engaging the devotional on page 59.

› Connect with God each day through prayer.

PERSONAL STUDY

› Read and interact with "The Pitfalls of Leadership" on page 60.

› Read and interact with "Tearing Down Your Idols" on page 64.

APPLICATION

› Memorize Exodus 19:4-6: "You yourselves have seen what I did to the Egyptians, and how I bore you on eagles' wings and brought you to myself. Now therefore, if you will indeed obey my voice and keep my covenant, you shall be my treasured possession among all peoples, for all the earth is mine; and you shall be to me a kingdom of priests and a holy nation."

› Update your journal by writing down some of the self-doubts that are preventing you from taking more of a leadership role in your home, school, or church. For each doubt you list, journal how God might respond to you like He did to Moses in Exodus 3.

› Connect with a close friend this week either in person, on the phone, or through text or social media. Share some of the things you've learned so far in this study or even some of the things you've written in your personal journal. When we share how God is working in our lives, God uses it to work in the lives of others.

READ

Read through the following Scripture passages this week.
Use the space provided to record your thoughts and responses.

Day 1: Exodus 2

Day 2: Exodus 3

Day 3: Exodus 4

Day 4: Exodus 16

Day 5: Exodus 17

Day 6: Numbers 14

Day 7: Numbers 20:1-13

REFLECT

GOD-HONORING RELUCTANCE

Moses was reluctant when God first called him to lead the people of Israel out of Egypt. But his reluctance was dishonoring to God because it was focused more on his limitations than his Creator's power.

Read Exodus 4:10-11.

You'd think after seeing God perform so many signs and wonders in delivering the people of Israel out of Egypt, that Moses would've transformed into the most confident leader imaginable. But when God called him to lead the people into the promised land, Moses was reluctant once again.

His initial reluctance was driven by doubt, but this time it was an expression of humility and dependence upon God.

> "If your presence will not go with me, do not bring us up from here."
> **Exodus 33:15**

Moses took his eyes off himself and asked God to show him His "glory" (33:18). Whereas God had expressed His anger to Moses at his initial reluctance (4:14), God revealed "His goodness" to him in a mysterious, but physical way (33:19-23).

When you face a decision about whether or not to take action, consider whether or not any hesitation is coming from doubt or dependence.

Ask God to show you His goodness, so that you might overcome any doubt-driven reluctance and desire nothing more than His presence and glory.

PERSONAL STUDY 1

- -

THE PITFALLS OF LEADERSHIP

At his lowest point as a leader (Num. 20:2-13), Moses disobeyed God and cursed the people. At Meribah, where God had previously provided water for the people, Moses strikes the rock with his staff, when God commanded him only to speak to it. As a result, Moses wasn't permitted to enter into the promised land.

Numbers 20 doesn't record for us a random, isolated incident, but rather the culminating expression of rage due to issues within Moses' heart left unresolved for too long. It was the eventual end result of a downward spiral through frustration, fatigue, loneliness, and bitterness—pitfalls common for all leaders.

FRUSTRATION

Frustration was a constant reality for Moses in his leadership. His frustration was a result of his own insecurity and the ongoing resistance of the people to God's plan. Over and over again, the people would complain to Moses about the lack of food and water. Often the people expressed their opposition by glorifying their life of slavery in Egypt.

> ³ "Would that we had died by the hand of the LORD in the land of Egypt, when we sat by the meat pots and ate bread to the full, for you have brought us out into this wilderness to kill this whole assembly with hunger."
> **Exodus 16:3**

Over and over again the people "grumbled against Moses" and complained about their circumstances (Ex. 15:24; 16:2; 17:3; Num. 11:1; 14:2). Few leaders in the Bible experienced this kind of constant resistance like Moses did (which is why none of that generation made it into the promised land).

How do you think you would have responded to all the grumbling and complaining if you were in Moses' situation?

How have you responded to resistance you've faced while trying to be a leader?

EXHAUSTION

When Jethro, Moses' father-in-law, visited Moses in the wilderness and saw him handling all the people's disputes from morning till evening, he responded:

> [17] "What you are doing is not good. [18] You and the people with you will certainly wear yourselves out, for the thing is too heavy for you. You are not able to do it alone."
> **Exodus 18:17-18**

Jethro knew that Moses was going to burn out if he didn't start handing over responsibility to other leaders. Moses listened to his father-in-law's advice and appointed others to deal with the small matters, while he judged the rest. Moses began sharing "the burden" (18:22) of leadership with others.

What is causing exhaustion in your life?

What "burdens" can you share with others?

LONELINESS

Exodus records only one instance of Moses experiencing true fellowship with God and a team of leaders after implementing Jethro's advice.

> [9] Then Moses and Aaron, Nadab, and Abihu, and seventy of the elders of Israel went up, [10] and they saw the God of Israel. There was under his feet as it were a pavement of sapphire stone, like the very haven for clearness. [11] And he did not lay his hand on the chief men of the people of Israel; they beheld God, and ate and drank.
> **Exodus 24:9-11**

From there Moses walked up the mountain to receive the tablets of stone that the law and commandments were written on (24:12). But while Moses was on the mountain for forty days and forty nights (24:18), the people grew restless and called upon Aaron, "Up, make us gods who shall go before us. As for this Moses, the man who brought us up out of the land of Egypt, we do not know that has become of him" (32:1). Aaron listened and directed the people in creating the golden calf.

The same leaders that Moses shared a meal with in the presence of God to confirm His covenant abandoned him. Aaron gave into the people's idolatry, and the elders did nothing to stop it. In Numbers 11:16-17, curiously similar to Exodus 18, God directs Moses to appoint seventy men to serve as elders and officers of the people. We are never told what happened to the first seventy elders, but it's safe to assume they were disqualified from leadership after the golden calf incident.

How have you experienced loneliness?

When have you felt abandoned by a friend or fellow leader?

BITTERNESS

Hard-pressed by frustration, exhaustion, and loneliness, Moses grows bitter. In Numbers 11, Moses begins expressing that bitterness. Not surprisingly, it happens during the complaints of the people:

> 11 Moses said to the LORD, "Why have you dealt ill with your servant? And why have I not found favor in your sight, that you lay the burden of all this people on me? 12 Did I conceive all this people? Did I give them birth, that you should say to me, 'Carry them in your bosom, as a nurse carries a nursing child,' to the land that you sword to give their fathers? 13 Where am I to get meat to give all this people? For they weep before me and say, 'Give us meat, that we may eat.'" 14 I am not able to carry all this people alone; the burden is too heavy for me. 15 If you will treat me like this, kill me at once, if I find favor in your sight, that I may no see my wretchedness."
> **Numbers 11:11-15**

In his bitterness, Moses does not see the situation with the right eyes. He takes the people's rejection personally, and fails to see that it is God they're reject. "The anger of the LORD blazed hotly, and Moses was displeased" (11:10) but for different reasons. As Old Testament scholar Timothy R. Ashley writes,

> "Moses does not react against the people's rejection of God's provision but against the people for making his job as a leader more difficult, and against Yahweh for giving him the task as a leader." [1]

In his bitterness, Moses could only see his frustration, exhaustion, and loneliness. He lost sight of all the extraordinary ways God had provided in the past. He cries out, "Where am I to get meat to give to all this people?" (11:13), having completely forgotten that God had already miraculously provided it for them in the past (Ex. 16)!

How can recalling how God has provided for you in the past encourage you when you are struggling with bitterness and anger?

List some ways God has blessed you in the past. What will you do to remember these blessings when you're tempted to forget His goodness?

PERSONAL STUDY 2

TEARING DOWN YOUR IDOLS

In his book *Counterfeit Gods*, Tim Keller writes, "To contemporary people the word idolatry conjures up pictures of primitive people bowing down before statues."[2] Given the difference between our culture and the Old Testament, we can read about the Israelites worship the golden calf (Ex. 32) and come away with the impression that idolatry is not a problem that an enlightened, modern society like ours deals with anymore.

But the idea of idolatry is so much more than giant golden calves and little figurines. In Romans 1, Paul gives a brief explanation of idolatry:

> 21 For although they knew God, they did not honor him as God or give thanks in him, but they became futile in their thinking, and their foolish hearts were darkened. 22 Claiming to be wise, they became fools, 23 and exchanged the glory of the immortal God for images resembling mortal man and birds and animals and reptiles.
> **Romans 1:21-23**

According to Paul, idolatry is taking anything in creation as an object of worship, instead of our Creator. We can make an idol out of anything.

There are a number of ways to identify idols in our lives, but there is one definition that Tim Keller provides that is particularly suited for understanding the root idolatry in both the people of Israel and in Moses during their wilderness wanderings. He writes:

> "A counterfeit god is anything so central and essential to your life that, should you lose it, your life would feel hardly worth living."[3]

Based on Keller's definition, what do you idolize?

THE ISRAELITES' IDOL

It may be difficult at first to recognize the root of the Israelites' because of how odd the golden calf may seem to us, but if we revisit the complaints they made towards God and Moses, it becomes a bit clearer that comfort was their primary idol. This idol says, "Life only has meaning [or]I only have worth if I have this kind of pleasure experience, a particular quality of life." [4] The Israelites often expressed this through their longings for food:

> [4] Now the rabble that was among them had a strong craving. And the people of Israel also wept again and said, "Oh that we had meat to eat! [5] We remember the fish we ate in Egypt that cost nothing, the cucumbers, the melons, the leeks, the onions, and the garlic. [6] But now our strength is dried up, and there is nothing at all but this manna to look at."
> **Numbers 11:4-6**

Time and time again, in complaining about their current situation, the Israelites would idealize Egypt. Notice how the people describe the fish as costing nothing and talk about their strength as now being dried up. In reality, that fish cost everything. They were slaves in Egypt who were constantly worked to the point of exhaustion.

The idol of comfort distorted their thinking to the point that they preferred slavery in Egypt above freedom in the promised land. The idol of comfort also prevented them from remembering all of the extraordinary ways that God provided for them—including their food and drink in the desert.

What "cravings" keep you from enjoying what God has already given you?

Whereas Israel, God's "son" (Ex. 4:22), complained about the food given to them, Jesus, the Son of God, told His disciples, "my food is to do the will of him who sent me and to accomplish his work" (John 4:24). Accomplishing the will of the Father meant great sacrifice on His part, and yet Jesus found satisfaction in fulfilling His mission.

How can the love of comfort prevent you from participating in God's redemptive mission in your life?

As believers, we can find strength to overcome the idolatry of comfort by remembering that Jesus is "the bread of Life" (John 6:48). Israel "ate the manna in the wilderness and died," but Jesus provides "the bread that comes down from heaven, so that one may eat of it and not die" (6:49-50). Through the power of the Holy Spirit, we can partake of "the living bread" (6:51), which reminds us that this life is not the end for us. God has an eternal plan for us that goes beyond this life.

MOSES' IDOLS

In our last study, we looked at a number of issues that contributed to the infamous Numbers 20 incident. While Moses was faithful to God in a way that the people never were, his disobedience in that moment cost him the opportunity to enter the promised land. There was an underlying idolatry in his own heart, as there is for each of us.

It is hard to identify the primary idol within Moses' heart, but it seems that approval was an issue for Moses. The idol of approval says, "Life only has meaning/I only have worth if I am loved and respected by this person."[5]

For those who struggle with approval, their greatest nightmare is rejection. It would seem that Moses was living his nightmare. As we looked at Numbers 11 in the previous study, we observed that Moses internalized the people's rejection of God's provision. How many times had the people complained against him? Enough to provoke Moses to ask that God take him out of his misery immediately (Num. 11:15).

It's also possible that Moses dealt with the idol of power, which says, "Life only has meaning/I only have worth if I have power and influence over others."[6] Any leader would have had difficulties leading the Israelites in those circumstances, but it seems that Moses was especially enraged by the hard-heartedness of the people. He certainly must have felt powerless dealing with constant complaints and rebellion. When he struck the rock and cursed the people at Meribah, he was trying to exert his own power and judgment apart from God.

Are approval and power idols for you? If so, how?

How do you typically handle rejection?

What is your typical response to situations that make you feel powerless?

It is hard to know what caused these idols to have sway over Moses' heart, but in part, we know that Moses questioned God's call from the very beginning. Even after seeing God perform several extraordinary signs, he still begged God to have someone join him before Pharaoh.

We can fight against approval and power by embracing the gospel truth that we are loved despite our performance because of Jesus' death in our place. We also see the gospel played out in the life of Jesus, the "prophet like Moses" (Acts 3:13-26; Deut. 18:15, 18), who before ever preaching a sermon or performing a miracle, received the Father's word of approval: "This is my beloved Son, with whom I am well pleased" (Matt. 3:17). As we embrace those words for ourselves through the gospel, we will find strength to turn away from our approval and power idols.

JOSHUA

SESSION 4

Joshua, who spent many years as Moses' assistant, was God's choice to lead the people into the promised land. The majority of passages that deal with Joshua reveal to us some important truths about leadership.

One of the primary lessons we learn from Joshua's life is that good leaders are willing to take risks.

In fact, risk is at the heart of Christianity.

Taking God at His word, Joshua was willing to trust that God would work for His people in extraordinary ways. Joshua was willing to stick his own neck out because he understood God's call.

But being a risk-taker didn't mean fear was absent from Joshua's heart. That's why God was constantly reminding him to be strong and courageous. Joshua needed to grow in these areas. He learned to be courageous as he drew closer to God in prayer—in both victory and defeat. As he reminded himself of God's promises over and over again, he gained strength.

Above all else, when we study Joshua's life, we discover that he was an exceptional leader because he was first and foremost a passionate worshiper.

START

- -

Welcome students back to the fourth group session.

Use the following to start your time together.

We're halfway through *Extraordinary: Extraordinary God, Ordinary People.* In the previous session we looked at how God worked through Moses despite his doubts. We also attempted to see deeper into Moses' frustration and failure.

> **As you completed your personal study of Session 3, what did you learn about overcoming insecurity and dealing with what's going on underneath the surface?**

> **What was it like for God's people to hold onto His promise in Exodus 33:14, "My presence will go with you, and I will give you rest"?**

Over these last few sessions, we've traced this process of "leaving" our comfort and doubts behind in order to lead. During this session, we're going to look at how God defines leadership and what it takes to join in His redemptive mission. Let's listen to Darrin on the leadership of Joshua, Moses' successor.

Pray for God to open your hearts and minds before showing the video for Session 4.

WATCH

Use the space below to follow along and take notes as you watch the video for Session 4.

1. _____ is at the heart of Christianity.

2. Just because Joshua was a risk-taker didn't mean he didn't have _____.

3. Fear is empowered by _____.

4. Community creates _____.

5. Step up and present yourself as a _____.

Scriptures: Numbers 13, 14:10; Joshua 1:9, 6, 10, 24:15; Matthew 9:37-38; Hebrews 11:1

1. Risk 2. fear 3. lies 4. courage 5. leader

DISCUSS

Use the following statements and questions below to discuss the Session 4 video.

Let's begin where Darrin began by answering these questions:

When have you been in a situation where you needed a leader?

In those situations, do you tend to step up right away or wait for someone else to take charge?

Now Joshua stepped into a leadership position that had been held by Moses. Even though God did not permit Moses to lead the people into the promised land, he did extraordinary things as a leader.

When have you felt like you were in the shadow of someone else (A family member, friend, etc.)?

One of the first things we find out about Joshua was that he and Caleb were the only spies who gave a "good report" about the land when Moses sent them to investigate it for Israel. Joshua and Caleb saw the same land as the other 10 spies did. What distinguished them from the others was their willingness to trust God and look at the situation with the eyes of leaders. Let's read together how they responded to the people's desire to return to Egypt.

Read aloud Numbers 14:6-9.

What stands out to you about Joshua and Caleb's reaction?

Let's consider how Darrin compared leaders and non-leaders:

1. Leaders step up when the situation looks bleak. Non-leaders bail.
2. Leaders are driven by opportunity. Non-leaders are driven by environment.
3. Leaders are led by the voice of God. Non-leaders are led by the voice of people.

Which one of these descriptions grabs your attention the most and why?

Darrin said that "risk is at the heart of Christianity" and that "faith is always a risk."

How do these phrases challenge you in your personal walk with Christ?

What are some examples of risks that you or people you know have taken in order to follow Jesus?

What is the connection between risk and prayer?

In addition to being willing to take risks, Darrin said that good leaders learn to be courageous. This comes about through one's own devotion to God, but it is also learned through community.

When have you faced a risky step of faith and needed the support and encouragement of close friends or family?

How did this community of friends or family give you encouragement or support to help you face a situation?

What have you found challenging, encouraging, or insightful from this session's study of Joshua?

Conclude your group time with the prayer activity on the following page. Complete the personal study for Session 4 before the next session.

PRAY

Darrin identified three lies that empower fear:

1. I can't be like _____.

2. God can't use me right now.

3. I can't influence people.

Which of these lies are you most likely to believe?

In the coming days, pay close attention to the times when you sense yourself giving into one of the three lies (or a similar one).

Use these occasions as opportunities to connect with God in prayer and to connect with a family member, friend, or someone in this group for encouragement.

As you take prayer requests and close in prayer, consider how God has ideally situated you to step up and lead in certain areas of your life.

PRAYER REQUESTS

MOVING FURTHER

In addition to studying God's Word, work with your group leader to create a plan for worship, personal study, and application between now and the next session. Select from the following optional activities to match your personal preferences and available time.

WORSHIP

> Read your Bible. Complete the reading plan on page 76.

> Spend time with God by engaging the devotional on page 77.

> Connect with God each day through prayer.

PERSONAL STUDY

> Read and interact with "How Godly Leaders Are Developed" on page 78.

> Read and interact with "How God's Leaders Show Courage" on page 82.

APPLICATION

> Find a parent, your group leader, or pastor to talk to this week. Whether you are currently leading something or not, ask them what they think the next step in your growth and leadership might be.

> Memorize Joshua 1:9: "Have I not commanded you? Be strong and courageous. Do not be frightened, and do not be dismayed, for the LORD your God is with you wherever you go."

> Do a prayer walk around your church or school (you do not need to pray out loud), asking God to open an opportunity for you to get to know a church member or classmate better and to give you the courage to engage him or her in a spiritual conversation.

READ

**Read through the following Scripture passages this week.
Use the space provided to record your thoughts and responses.**

Day 1: Exodus 17:8-15; 33:7-11

Day 2: Numbers 13

Day 3: Deuteronomy 34; Joshua 1:1-9

Day 4: Joshua 4

Day 5: Joshua 6

Day 6: Joshua 23

Day 7: Joshua 24

REFLECT

THE COMMANDER OF THE LORD'S ARMY

Just after Joshua led the people across the Jordan River into the promised land, before they engaged in any battles, he had an extraordinary encounter.

> When Joshua was by Jericho, he lifted up his eyes and looked, and behold, a man was standing before him with his drawn sword in his hand. And Joshua went to him and said to him, "Are you for us, or for our adversaries?" 14 And he said, "No; but I am the commander of the army of the Lord. Now I have come." And Joshua fell on his face to the earth and worshiped and said to him, "What does my lord say to his servant?" 15 And the commander of the Lord's army said to Joshua, "Take off your sandals from your feet, for the place where you are standing is holy." And Joshua did so.
> **Joshua 5:13-15**

Joshua responded in worship to this mysterious man, whose presence makes the place they are standing holy. Many believe this is an early appearance of Christ in human history.

Though in this situation Joshua was pursuing the clear will of God, it wouldn't always be that way for the people of Israel. They regularly used their status as God's chosen people to try and justify their sin. They wrongly believed that their covenant with God meant He would endorse their plans. They failed to see that this covenant meant God was committed to their ultimate good, not simply "the good" they wanted for themselves. Joshua was used greatly by God because he was more than a leader. Joshua was first and foremost a worshiper.

Take time now to consider the things in your life you're pursuing. Do you simply follow God so that He will bless your plans, or are you worshiping God with open hands, allowing His will to be done in and through your life?

PERSONAL STUDY 1

HOW GODLY LEADERS ARE DEVELOPED

The Book of Joshua begins with his appointment as the new leader of the people of Israel, and it traces his leadership from that point until his death. The book ends by giving Joshua the highest praise any leader could receive.

> Israel served the LORD all the days of Joshua, and all the days of the elders who outlived Joshua and had known all the work that the LORD did for Israel.
> **Joshua 24:31**

But well before Joshua was a "successful" leader, when he was still a young man, he served as Moses' "assistant" (Ex. 24:13). The Bible does not specifically call Moses a "mentor" to Joshua, but we can deduce that from their close relationship. When we look back through the Books of Exodus, Numbers, and Deuteronomy, we get a glimpse of Joshua's development as a leader underneath Moses' mentorship.

The Bible doesn't provide us with a clear, step-by-step guide to leadership development, but there are at least three observations we can make about what good mentors do by looking at Moses and Joshua's relationship.

FIRST, GOOD MENTORS PROVIDE RELATIONSHIP.

In last session's first personal study, we read about the meal that Moses had with the leaders of Israel (Ex. 24:9-11). This wasn't just about food; it was about fellowship—with God and with one another.

Immediately after "they beheld God, and ate and drank," the Lord calls Moses. Notice who accompanies him. "So Moses rose with his assistant Joshua, and Moses went up into the mountain of God" (24:13). This verse seems to indicate that Joshua took part in that fellowship meal with the "chief men of the people of Israel" (24:11)—even though Joshua was not numbered as one of the elders. Moses brought Joshua into that experience. Moses gave Joshua unprecedented access.

Do you have a mentor of any kind. If so, how has this relationship been helpful?

If you don't have a mentor, what would you want to gain from one?

SECOND, GOOD MENTORS PROVIDE RESPONSIBILITY.

Some people struggle to develop into the leaders they could be because they're never really put into challenging situations. They may be given some small tasks to do, but nothing of great consequence. Moses, on the other hand, gave Joshua a big responsibility at a young age. The first time we come across Joshua in the Bible is in Exodus 17:9. This chapter records the first battle that Moses and the people of Israel experience after being delivered from Egypt.

> 8 Then Amalek came and fought with Israel at Rephidim.
> 9 So Moses said to Joshua, "Choose for us men, and go out and fight with Amalek. Tomorrow I will stand on the top of the hill with the staff of God in my hand." 10 So Joshua did as Moses told him, and fought with Amalek, while Moses, Aaron, and Hur went up to the top of the hill.
> **Exodus 17:8-10**

If you were in Joshua's shoes, how would you have responded to this request?

By taking on this responsibility, Joshua gained experience that clearly prepared him for leading Israel in the future. By submitting to Moses' direction, Joshua saw God up close fighting for them in an extraordinary and mysterious way (the raised staff of Moses, Ex. 17:11-13).

What big responsibilities have you been given in the past? What did you learn through that process?

THIRD, GOOD MENTORS PROVIDE CORRECTION.

In Numbers 11, God tells Moses to appoint elders to share in the burden of leading the people. God blesses these men with His empowering Spirit. As a result, the men begin prophesying, while before Moses had been the only one to do so. Hearing about this, Joshua says, "My lord Moses, stop them." Moses responds:

> "Are you jealous for my sake? Would that all the LORD's people were prophets, that the LORD would put his Spirit on them!"
> **Numbers 11:29**

Joshua may have thought he was looking out for his mentor, but his protest revealed a mixture of self-protection and jealousy. Though Moses had expressed his displeasure with God shortly before this, he responded with the attitude of a godly leader—to see more leaders developed who know God more intimately and are used by Him. Moses corrected Joshua's concern to protect Moses' (unique) position and by extension Joshua's own.

> **When is it difficult to embrace what God is doing in the lives of those around you?**

> **When have you been tempted to be jealous of God's work in someone else's life?**

> **What attitudes in your own heart need correction from God?**

Now that we've considered three things (*relationship, responsibility*, and *correction*) that good mentors give to emerging leaders, we need to observe the most significant aspect of leadership development—and it's something that good mentees (*those being mentored*) do.

GOOD MENTEES LOVE GOD MORE THAN THEY LOVE LEADING.

Despite Moses' failings as a leader, he had an extraordinary relationship with God. "The LORD used to speak to Moses face to face as a man speaks to his friend" (Ex. 33:11a). But notice the second half of the verse:

> When Moses turned again into the camp, his assistant Joshua the son of Nun, a young man would depart from the tent.
> **Exodus 33:11b**

The "tent of meeting" was the early version of the temple and was a place of worship. It was where the people went to meet with God—primarily mediated through Moses and the priests. Some suggest that Joshua stayed in the tent of meeting to guard it in Moses' absence, but it certainly would have meant more than that for him.

Earlier, he had accompanied Moses up the mountain where God spoke with Moses (Ex. 24:13). Being near God was not a task, but a privilege.

What are some examples of someone loving leading more than loving God?

How can you avoid making your mentor(s) a substitute for God?

What are you doing to experience God's presence on a regular basis?

No matter how godly the people are in your life, no relationship is more important than your personal relationship with the Lord. Your goal should not be to become more like any man or woman, but rather more like Christ.

Take time to prayerfully consider who can help you grow as a Christian and as a leader—stepping up within your own circle of influence.

Pray about a person or small group of people God has put on your heart to either be mentored by or to mentor in your life. Everyone should always have someone who is pouring into their lives along with someone they are pouring into, no matter how young or old you are.

PERSONAL STUDY 2

HOW GOD'S LEADERS SHOW COURAGE

Three times (in eight verses), God tells Joshua to be "strong and courageous" as He confirms him as leader of the people of Israel. God ends His commissioning speech with a command of encouragement and a promise.

> Do not be frightened and do not be dismayed, for the LORD your God is with you wherever you go.
> **Joshua 1:9**

Fear was a natural response to what Joshua was about to undertake—leading the people of Israel in conquest of the promised land of Canaan. But to calm Joshua's fear, God promised to be with him and reassured him.

> "No man shall be able to stand before you all the days of your life. Just as I was with Moses, so I will be with you. I will not leave you or forsake you."
> **Joshua 1:5**

In addition to promising His presence, God gave Joshua specific instructions. Given the amount of attention given to battles and inheritance in the Book of Joshua, this is probably not the kind of instruction you would expect:

> [6] Be strong and courageous, for you shall cause this people to inherit the land that I swore to their fathers to give them. [7] Only be strong and very courageous, being careful to do according to all the law that Moses my servant commanded you. Do not turn from it to the right hand or to the left, that you may have good success wherever you go. [8] This book of the Law shall not depart from your mouth, but you shall meditate on it day and night, so that you may be careful to do according all that is written in it. For then you will make your way prosperous, and then you will have good success.
> **Joshua 1:6-8**

How does God define strength and courage for Joshua?

The key to Joshua's success in leading was his obedience to the book of the Law. God tells Joshua to meditate on it constantly ("day and night"), so that it would shape all his thoughts and actions. The "book of the Law" was God's covenant with Israel, specifically referring to the whole of Deuteronomy chapters 5-6 (including the blessings and curses of chapters 27 and 28), which Moses wrote down and read before the people.

The discipline of meditation (which included reading, praying, memorizing, and reflecting on God's law) was not merely a private spiritual exercise, but a vitally important habit that affected not just the life of a leader, but all under their leadership.

When do you spend time reflecting on God's Word?

Why is it important to have a consistent devotional time?

How does a regular time of personal devotion affect your daily life?

"Meditation" can be a loaded word. Many think of mystical religions or some process of emptying the mind. But biblical meditation is about filling the mind, specifically with thoughts on who God is and what He has done in order that we might gain the strength and courage needed to follow Him.

How has the Holy Spirit used God's Word in your life to impact the lives of those around you at home, school, or at practice?

Even with an accurate view of biblical meditation, it may be hard to understand how God's specific command for Joshua to meditate on "the book of the Law" would translate into strength and courage. The idea of meditating on the Law may seem more drudgery than delight. It is common for us to have a negative view of the Law. Often, we transfer our understanding of the scribes and Pharisees in Jesus' day as self-righteous onto all of the Old Testament saints. There is so much that can be said regarding the heart of God's Law—more than our space here permits— but there are two key elements of "the book of the Law" to observe.

First, "the book of the Law" does not actually begin with commands. It begins by acknowledging God's saving work:

> "I am the LORD your God, who brought you out of
> the land of Egypt, out of the house of slavery."
> **Deuteronomy 5:6**

Before the cross, the exodus was the defining act of salvation for God's people.

Why is it important that the Law begins this way?

Second, "the book of Law" was not only meant to shape Israel's relationship with God, but also their witness to the rest of the world.

> 6 "Keep them and do them, for that will be your wisdom and your understanding in the sight of all people, who, when they hear all theses statutes, will say, 'Surely this great nation is a wise and understanding people.' 7 For what great nation is there that has a god so near to it as the LORD our God is to us, whenever we call upon him? 8 And what great nation is there, that has statutes and rules so righteous as all this law that I set before you today."
> **Deuteronomy 4:6-8**

How does this passage affect your understanding of God's Law?

Compare verses 7 and 8. What is the connection between God's presence ("nearness") and the giving of the Law?

When we keep these two passages in view, we notice that the Book of Law both points back to God's rescue of His people from bondage (*salvation*) and points forward to His call of the people to be a light to all other nations (*mission*). Their obedience was motivated from salvation and for mission. The Law did not in itself have ability to supply Joshua with strength and courage, but it pointed to the Lawgiver, who was with him and for him.

JOB

SESSION 5

There is nothing more certain in a world stained by sin and permeated with brokenness than suffering. We know this to be true, and yet it doesn't prevent us from experiencing doubt and confusion when we actually suffer.

It doesn't help when the common responses to suffering are that life is random or that our suffering is deserved.

Job dealt with both those responses from his wife and "friends," eventually crying out to God for explanation, "Why?"

Job never gets his question answered, but he does get God. Even without an answer, he encounters God in such a powerful way that he repents of his attempts at self-justification. As his world was crumbling apart, Job discovered that God's presence was enough.

Through Job's story, we get a glimpse of what it means to be a good counselor to those as they suffering and are confronted with the fact that everything we have is a gift from God. We didn't earn it and we can't control it. But as we hold it all with open hands, we can see God more clearly than ever—even on account of our suffering.

START

- -

Welcome everyone back to the fifth group session.

Use the following to start your time together.

Over the last two sessions, we've looked at two major leaders from the Old Testament: Moses, who led the people out of bondage in Egypt, and Joshua, who led the people into the promised land. Through these men, we've considered some major themes regarding leadership: *doubt, fear, trust, courage,* and *obedience.*

> **Since the last session, what have you discovered about the character of a godly leader?**

> **What's one thing you've learned in our study so far that you are trying to apply in your life (at home, school, practice, etc.)?**

At some point in our lives, we realize that things don't always go well. God's favor doesn't always seem to look like blessing, influence, and success. So, what do we do when things don't seem to go right? Does that mean we're doing something wrong? Do bad things really happen to good people?

Given how much we've talked about God's promises and provisions over the last four sessions, we need to spend some time dealing with suffering—the primary focus in the Book of Job.

Pray for God to open your hearts and minds before showing the video for Session 5.

WATCH

Use the space below to follow along and take notes as you watch video Session 5.

1. When people suffer, they try to _____.

2. We all try to make a case for why we shouldn't be _____.

3. It's good to ask God _____ as long as you're OK with getting a _____ back.

4. Sometimes people don't need your _____, they just need _____.

5. Job never got an _____ or vindication, but he did get _____.

6. You know you're seeing _____ when you see everything in your life as _____.

Scriptures: Job 1-2, 4, 9, 38-42

1. simplify 2. suffering 3. questions, question 4. advice, you 5. explanation, God 6. God, grace

DISCUSS

Use the following statements and questions below to discuss the video.

Both inside and outside of the church we find a variety of responses to suffering, but Darrin identified two main ones:

1. A humanist says "life is random," so suffering is random.
2. A moralist says "life is cause and effect," so suffering is deserved.

When you see or experience suffering, which of these is your first response?

If you go back and forth between the two, what explains the shift?

Darrin compared the humanist response to Job's wife, "Do you still hold fast your integrity? Curse God and die" (Job 2:9). Then he compared the moralist response with Job's friends (Eliphaz, Bildad, and Zophar), "Who that was innocent ever perished? Or where were the upright cut off?" (Job 4:7)

Job described his wife (*the humanist*) as a foolish woman (Job 2:10) and his friends (*the moralists*) as "worthless physicians" (13:4).

Why is the humanist response "foolish" and the moralist response "worthless"?

Darrin explained that one of the results of personal suffering is that it can make us good counselors.

How can your suffering help you minister to someone else? How has someone else ministered to you through their quiet presence?

How has someone else's empathy through similar suffering allowed them to comfort you in your struggles?

When has someone's advice or explanation been hurtful rather than helpful in a time of suffering or confusion?

Have you ever sat quietly with someone who was suffering? How difficult was it to be silent? What were some of the challenges?

Darrin told us that there were two things Job wanted from God in his suffering—vindication and explanation. He wanted to hear that he did nothing wrong (and wanted his "friends" to hear that too) and he wanted to know why this was happening to him. God responds to Job, but God never answers the *why* question.

What do you think drives us to ask *why*?

What are we hoping to find out by asking?

Darrin mentioned two other fruits of suffering: *that we can see God more clearly* and *that we can be transformed by grace*. Though Job did not receive the reply he was expecting, he did get something extraordinary.

Read aloud Job 38:1-11.

Summarize what you think God's purpose was with His response. How is His response "grace" to Job?

How does God's response encourage you in your own suffering?

Read Job's response to God in Job 42:5-6.

How did Job's view of God change? How does this change Job's response to his own suffering?

When have you experienced God in a different way while suffering?

What else have you found challenging, encouraging, or insightful from this study of Job?

Conclude your group time with the prayer activity on the following page. Complete the personal study for Session 5 before the next session.

PRAY

In Job, we see someone who suffered immensely and never found out why he suffered, but experienced God in an extraordinary way that he had never seen before. Beholding God in this way did not remove his pain, but it did transform him.

Are you, or someone you know, currently in a painful situation for which the people in this group can pray or quietly comfort? Explain.

Read 1 Peter 5:6-11.

In our personal study this week, we're going to look at the primary way God speaks to us in our pain and suffering through the life and death of Jesus, the Son of God, who was there when the Father "laid the foundations of the earth" (Job 38:4).

As you take prayer requests and close in prayer, ask the Holy Spirit to help you endure your own pain and to comfort others who are suffering.

PRAYER REQUESTS

MOVING FURTHER

In addition to studying God's Word, work with your group leader to create a plan for worship, personal study, and application between now and the next session. Select from the following optional activities to match your personal preferences and available time.

WORSHIP

> Read your Bible. Complete the reading plan on page 94.

> Spend time with God by engaging the devotional on page 95.

> Connect with God each day through prayer.

PERSONAL STUDY

> Read and interact with "God's Purpose for Our Suffering" on page 96.

> Read and interact with "God's Own Experience of Suffering" on page 100.

APPLICATION

> Make a list of people you personally know who are dealing with pain and loss right now. Spend some time praying for them, and as the Spirit guides you, write them a note or send them a text to let them know that you are praying for them.

> Read through all of God's response to Job in chapters 38-41. Consider reading it aloud as a way to increase your concentration on the text.

> Memorize Job 42:5-6: "I had heard of you by the hearing of my ear, but now my eyes see you; therefore I despise myself, and repent in dust and ashes."

> Continue writing in your journal by acknowledging some personal suffering that caused (and may still cause) you to question God's goodness. Ask God to help you make sense of that experience or find peace apart from explanation.

READ

Read through the following Scripture passages this week. Use the space provided to record your thoughts and responses.

Day 1: Job 1

Day 2: Job 2

Day 3: Job 8-9

Day 4: Job 13

Day 5: Job 23

Day 6: Job 38

Day 7: Job 42

REFLECT

POETIC LAMENT

The Book of Job is narrative unlike what we've come across in Genesis through Joshua. It is best understood as wisdom literature, a genre of Scripture that includes Psalms, Proverbs, and Ecclesiastes. Some also find similarities within Song of Solomon, Ruth, and Lamentations. Many of these books are more poetic than prosaic in nature. We are not meant to merely search for the doctrine, but to consider the vast range of human emotion that is given voice.

Consider the fact that God has chosen to reveal Himself through a variety of literary genres. He cares not only about history and law, but also about emotion and beauty. He desires to relate to us in every part of our being.

Job's speeches take the form of poetic lament. In form and style they resemble the laments found in the Psalms, which have been considered the prayer book or songbook of God's people. It is interesting that laments are one of the most frequent types of psalms. Old Testament scholar Tremper Longman describes the laments as "the psalmist's cry when in great distress he has nowhere to turn but God."[1]

Longman identifies three kinds of complaints found with the laments: (1) trouble over one's own thoughts and actions, (2) trouble over the actions of others against the psalmist, and (3) frustration with God Himself.[2] It is remarkable, if not shocking, to see such raw intensity and honesty within the Book of Job and the lament psalms. God is not only OK with our honest emotions, Scripture reveals that they are part of genuine relationship with God. See Psalm 10, 31, 39, 55, 77, and 142 for examples of lament.

Spend time prayerfully considering your own feelings, questions, or suffering. Voice these things to God. Consider writing your own psalm of lament.

PERSONAL STUDY 1

GOD'S PURPOSE FOR OUR SUFFERING

The Bible is full of tensions—two truths that seem contradictory on the surface, but are in fact complementary. The tension regarding suffering is that it is both mysterious and meaningful.

In his book *Walking with God through Pain and Suffering,* Tim Keller writes:

> "Christianity teaches that, contra fatalism, suffering is overwhelming; contra Buddhism, suffering is real; contra karma, suffering is often unfair; but contra secularism, suffering is meaningful. There is a purpose to it, and if faced rightly, it can drive us like a nail deep into the love of God and into more stability and spiritual power than you can imagine."[3]

In our group time, we discussed how suffering can help us see God more clearly. We considered how Job was changed by his encounter with God (though it was not what he expected):

> [2] "I know that you can do all things, and that no purpose of yours can be thwarted. [3] 'Who is this that hides counsel without knowledge?' Therefore I have uttered what I did not understand, things too wonderful for me, which I did not know. [4] 'Hear, and I will speak; I will question you, and you make it known to me.' [5] I had heard of you by the hearing of the ear, but now my eyes see you; [6] therefore I despise myself, repent in dust and ashes."
> **Job 42:2-6**

Due to its poetic nature and its position within God's special revelation (Scripture), the Book of Job is more concerned with depicting rather than explaining the change that takes place through Job's suffering. We turn to the New Testament Epistles, written in light of Jesus' incarnation, death, and resurrection, for more explanation on one purpose of suffering.

Read the following passages of Scripture and record how they contribute to your understanding of the purpose of suffering:

Romans 5:3-5

James 1:2-4

1 Peter 1:6-7

The passage in 1 Peter provides us the most vivid comparison for suffering. Our faith is compared to gold, a precious metal, that is exposed to extreme heat in order to remove its impurities. The fire is not intended to destroy, but refine the precious metal. Peter is saying, in the same way, trials are meant to shape our faith into its most purest form.

How have you seen or personally experienced trials that produce a greater, more pure faith?

What kinds of "impurities" do you think God is trying to remove from you through trials?

In these three passages, we are encouraged to "rejoice" in our sufferings. The point is not that we are meant to enjoy our pain, but to take joy in what the trial will produce in us. That is why our future hope is found within the surrounding context:

> 2 Through him we have also obtained access by faith into this grace in which we stand, and we rejoice in hope of the glory of God.
> **Romans 5:2**

> 12 Blessed is the man who remains steadfast under trial, for when he has stood the test he will receive the crown of life, which God has promised to those who love him.
> **James 1:12**

> 3 Blessed be the God and Father of our Lord Jesus Christ! According to his great mercy, he has caused us to be born again to a living hope through the resurrection of Jesus Christ from the dead, 4 to an inheritance that is imperishable, undefiled, and unfading, kept in heaven for you,
> **1 Peter 1:3-4**

How can you remind yourself of your future hope as a motivation for remaining steadfast through your trials and suffering?

What would it look like for you to embrace the trials that God brings into your life? Or to put it another way, what does it look like when you try to avoid God's refining process?

Close your time of study by praying for God to help you to embrace His transformative work in you through suffering. This doesn't mean trials are less painful or confusing. Trusting God in the midst of suffering means you are hopeful and believe that He will ultimately use the experience for good.

PERSONAL STUDY 2

GOD'S OWN EXPERIENCE OF SUFFERING

As we saw in this session's reflection, various genres of literature are used to connect with people in different ways. Genre and language highlight different elements and nuances that reveal what the author—God through different people at different times in the case of Scripture—desires to communicate.

Word choice is just as important in contemporary culture as it was in ancient times. Language is rich in communicating not only facts, but also values. Often different cultures will have multiple words to emphasize what may seem to others as subtle nuance. These distinctions help draw attention to something specific that is important to the communicator even if someone would otherwise understand the general meaning.

For example, it's interesting that the French language has two words for what we'd simply translate as *knowing*.

One word is *savoir*, which refers to knowing about something or knowing how to do something.

The other word is *connaitre*, which refers to knowing someone.

This distinction, which is lacking in the English language, is useful as we consider what resources we have in Christianity for dealing with suffering.

In the previous personal study, while talking about the meaning and purpose to suffering, we focused more on the first type of knowing. It was about knowing the nature of the process. But if we just stop there, we may find the Christian response to be intellectually satisfying, but not altogether comforting. The unique resource we have for dealing with suffering is Jesus Himself. God does not just know about pain, God has experienced pain. The pain of the cross is forever a part of the Trinity's memory.

The Book of Job (just like the entire Old Testament) points to Christ. While Job was a relatively innocent suffer, Jesus is the ultimate Job, the only truly innocent sufferer. Apart from the passion narratives in the Gospels, few describe Jesus' suffering as vividly as the prophet Isaiah:

> ³ He was despised and rejected by men;
> a man of sorrows, and acquainted with grief;
> and as one from whom men hide their faces
> he was despised, and we esteemed him not.
> ⁴ Surely he has borne our griefs
> and carried our sorrows;
> yet we esteemed him stricken,
> smitten by God, and afflicted.
> ⁵ But he was perceived for our transgressions;
> he was crushed for our iniquities;
> upon his was the chastisement that brought us peace,
> and with his wounds we are healed.
> **Isaiah 53:3-5**

How does this passage stir you to worship and allow you to better understand God as the Suffering Servant?

What difference does it make that we worship a God in Jesus who was "a man of sorrows, and acquainted with grief" (53:3)?

The very next line of this "Suffering Servant" passage displays another reason why Jesus is the ultimate Job:

> 7 He was oppressed, and he was afflicted,
> yet he opened not his mouth;
> like a lamb that is led to the slaughter,
> and like a sheep that before its shearers is silent,
> so he opened not his mouth.
> **Isaiah 53:7**

While Job sought to defend himself before God, Jesus willingly endured suffering so that we might have peace with God. Jesus knew why His suffering was necessary and what it would produce. In one sense this was crucial. Hebrews says it was "for the joy that was set before him" that Jesus "endured the cross" (12:2). But the meaningfulness did not remove the agonizing pain.

Read the following gospel accounts of Jesus in Gethsemane. How is the humanity of Jesus expressed in each one? What emotions and pains did Jesus experience as He approached His death?

Matthew 26:36-46

Mark 14:32-42

Luke 22:39-46

Gethsemane would not be the last time Jesus prayed to God the Father before His death. On the cross, Jesus spoke the words:

> "My God, my God, why have you forsaken me?"
> **Matthew 27:47**

These are the opening words to Psalm 22. Read it if you have a few minutes. This psalm of David not only expressed feelings about his own circumstances, but it also prophetically pointed toward Jesus and His experience in crucifixion.

In His time of greatest agony, He offered up the lament of an innocent sufferer. In our time of need, we can offer up our own laments knowing that we have a God who can sympathize with us, having experienced it Himself.

If you didn't write out a psalm of lament during the reflection portion of this session, consider doing so now. If you did, consider writing another one, pouring out your heart to God, knowing that He has suffered pain, and placing your hope in Jesus.

ESTHER

SESSION 6

The story of Esther shows us that God isn't just in the big and spectacular, but the small and ordinary. Not once is God ever explicitly mentioned, but there are evidences of His invisible hand all throughout the book.

Esther isn't the picture of a perfect hero, but she is a timely one. The chain of events that led to her becoming queen was essentially beyond her control. The decisions she did make were often morally questionable but based on self-preservation.

When she realized that perhaps God had orchestrated it all for her to intervene on behalf of God's people, she changed. Realizing she had a role in what God was doing in the world, Esther put her life on the line.

Esther's story gives us confidence that God can use us to impact the lives of others as we consider the positions of influence we've been placed and the needs around us.

More than that, Esther points to Jesus, who gave up the ultimate position in the ultimate palace, and laid down His life, so that we might be free from the enemies that try to destroy us.

START

Welcome students back to the final group session.

Use the following to start your time together.

We have arrived at our final session of *Extraordinary: Extraordinary God, Ordinary People*. Last session, we explored the topic of suffering through the Book of Job, which seemingly calls into question the goodness and character of God. And yet we considered how Job pointed us to the ultimate Job, Jesus, the only truly innocent sufferer.

Are you beginning to see God in a new light? If so, how?

Did anyone write their own psalm of lament? Would anyone like to share a lament they wrote or what they gained from the experience of being honest about their feelings with God?

In the last five sessions, we've studied the lives of people who experienced God in direct and amazing ways. But few of us encounter God in such miraculous ways. So, how do we respond when God seems distant?

In our final session, Darrin is going walk us through the Book of Esther—a book of the Bible that surprisingly never mentions the name of God.

Pray for God to open your hearts and minds before showing the video for Session 6.

WATCH

Use the space below to follow along and take notes as you watch video Session 6.

1. God uses Esther in her _____.

2. _____ causes us to constantly ask ourselves _____ questions.

3. A humble person is more interested in _____ you than _____ _____ by you.

4. God is at work _____ _____ _____.

5. Your talents and opportunities were _____ to you so that God can _____ you.

Scriptures: Esther; Matthew 4:19

DISCUSS

Use the following statements and questions below to discuss the video.

Darrin recounted much of Esther's story. There was a lot in the video, so you'll read through the entire book (just 10 chapters) in your personal study.

Summarize the plot of Esther. What were the key points?

Esther is an unlikely hero. She's living in exile as an orphan who was taken against her will (as Esther 2:8 suggests) into a pagan king's harem.

On a scale of 0-10 (0 being *none* and 10 being *total*), how would you rate her influence over her situation at the beginning of the story? At the end of the story? Explain your ratings and any change?

0   1   2   3   4   5   6   7   8   9   10

Twice we read that Esther concealed her Jewish identity while in the harem at the command of Mordecai (Esth. 2:10, 20). It seems that she went along with every aspect of the "beauty pageant."

Did she do the right thing in her situation? Why or why not?

Without knowing the end of the story, what would you have done?

What does God's plan to use Esther to save His people say about His character?

After Haman is promoted to the king's right hand, he has an encounter with Mordecai. Because Mordecai, revealing his Jewishness, will not bow down and pay homage, Haman is "filled with fury" (3:5). He plots to destroy all the Jews and successfully persuades the king to see them as a threat. Mordecai then appeals to Esther to use her position to save her people.

Read Esther 4:13-14.

If Mordecai believed that "relief and deliverance" would arise even if it didn't come through Esther, why did Esther risk her life?

Darrin used the question Mordecai posed to Esther as an entryway into discussing God's providence. The deliverance that God provides for His people was not obvious or spectacular, though it was still extraordinary.

How would you explain God's providence?

Looking back on your own life, how can you see God's hand bringing you to where you are today?

Darrin described Esther's appeal to the king as identification (*"I am one of them"*) and mediation (*"Do not harm them"*).

How is Esther's identification and mediation a picture of Jesus?

What would it look for you to identify as one of God's people in your home, school, or on a team?

How might you be in a position share the gospel?

What are some "ordinary events" that you've seen God use to bring healing in your family or your school?

What else has been challenging, encouraging, or insightful from this study of Esther?

As we conclude this study, what have you learned about God over the past six sessions? About your relationship with Him?

What has been the most practical takeaway to help you live out your faith in our extraordinary God?

Conclude your group time with the prayer activity on the following page. Complete the personal study for Session 6.

PRAY

- -

We may never find our lives at stake, but we do risk our reputation and even some relationships when we identify ourselves as followers of Jesus. We can only take these risks when we trust that God is at work in and around our lives—even when we can't see how.

Spend some time now sharing ways that God has been at work in your life since joining this small group. Journal about these here as well.

As we close out our time together, let's pray that God would help us see past all the things on the surface that would keep us from being used by Him. Let's ask the Holy Spirit to help us see the opportunities we have to be a blessing to others and a witness to the gospel of Jesus Christ.

PRAYER REQUESTS

MOVING FURTHER

In addition to studying God's Word, work with your group leader to create a plan for worship, personal study, and application in your daily life. Select from the following optional activities to match your personal preferences and available time.

WORSHIP

> Read your Bible. Complete the reading plan on page 112.

> Spend time with God by engaging the devotional on page 113.

> Connect with God each day through prayer.

PERSONAL STUDY

> Read and interact with "Acknowledging Our Identity" on page 114.

> Read and interact with "Providence and Responsibility" on page 118.

APPLICATION

> In a sentence, Esther is the story of a woman who exercised the influence afforded her position for the good of a vulnerable group of people. Make a list of all the positions of influence you hold (no matter how small they seem), whether you are a younger or older sibling or maybe a teammate to someone. Pray that the Spirit would reveal to you how you can better leverage your influence for the sake of God's kingdom.

> Memorize Esther 4:14: "For if you keep silent at this time, relief and deliverance will rise for the Jews from another place, but you and your father's house will perish. And who knows whether you have not come to the kingdom for such a time as this."

> As you read through the Book of Esther, write down all the "coincidences" you can find that point to God's providential care over Esther, Mordecai, and His people.

READ

Read through the following Scripture passages this week. Use the space provided to record your thoughts and responses.

Day 1: Esther 1-2

Day 2: Esther 3

Day 3: Esther 4

Day 4: Esther 5

Day 5: Esther 6

Day 6: Esther 7-8

Day 7: Esther 9-10

REFLECT

MY QUESTIONABLE PAST

Many of us live with the regret of our past decisions. We expend so much energy avoiding or numbing out our feelings of shame that we're unable to connect with God in the present. It often prevents us from taking risks because we doubt that God could—or even would—use us to make difference in the lives of people around us.

Esther's story can give us confidence that God not only uses us to change the lives of others, but He can do that through our questionable past. Her story can also give us confidence that God works even through the parts of our past that we had no control over. The word that Mordecai has for Esther may be the one God has for you:

> "Who knows whether you have not come to
> the kingdom for such a time as this?"
> **Esther 4:14**

Use the space below to consider what opportunities God has put in front of you to advance His kingdom. Pray and ask the Spirit to reveal to you any shame and regret from your past. Meditate on the verses below as you consider how to step out in faith.

> There is therefore now no condemnation
> for those who are in Christ Jesus.
> **Romans 8:1**

> For you did not receive the spirit of slavery to fall back
> into fear, but you have received the Spirit of adoption
> as sons, by whom we cry, "Abba! Father!"
> **Romans 8:15**

PERSONAL STUDY 1

ACKNOWLEDGING OUR IDENTITY

As a result of their constant unfaithfulness to the covenant, God judged the nation of Israel by removing them from the land. The Babylonian exile was God's means of judgment. Life outside the land raised many questions for the Jews. Had God given up on His people entirely? How were they to remain faithful in a new society and culture whose values were often directly opposed to God? What did it mean to identify as one of God's people now?

The Books of Esther and Daniel, exclusively concerned with the dealings of Jews during the exile, raise those important questions. Esther's own growth in courage was directly connected to her willingness to identify as Jewish. Shortly into her story, we discover that she has been advised by Mordecai to conceal her Jewish identity. We don't know the exact reason, but perhaps it was out of fear that she would be treated (even more) horribly as a foreigner (than what was already expected for a young girl within the king's harem). We do know that Esther had to reveal her identity to the king in order to intervene for God's people (Esth. 7:4).

In what ways are you pressured to conceal your Christian identity?

What are some of the costs associated with revealing your Christian identity?

Even though many Jews would eventually return to Jerusalem, the land would continue to be occupied by one world superpower after the next. The entire New Testament was written within the context of the Roman Empire's virtual world-wide rule. Many of the questions asked by Jews during the exile continued to be the questions asked by the early church.

The apostle Peter uses the language of "exile" in his letter (1 Pet. 1:1, 17), describing believers as "sojourners and exiles" (2:11). He did so to prepare the church for persecution they would experience by claiming "Jesus is Lord," not "Caesar is Lord." Though the apostle Paul does not use the explicit language of exile, he does play on the concept of citizenship.

> 17 Brothers, join in imitating me, and keep your eyes on those who walk according to the example you have in us. 18 For many, of whom I have often told you and now tell you even with tears, walk as enemies of the cross of Christ. 19 Their end is destruction, their god is their belly, and they glory in their shame, with minds set on earthly things. 20 But our citizenship is in heaven and from it we await a Savior, the Lord Jesus Christ,
> **Philippians 3:17-20**

What does it mean that "our citizenship is in heaven" (v. 20)?

According to Paul, how is that spiritual reality practically expressed in our lives?

The language we come across in passages like these draw clear distinctions between those who follow Jesus and those who reject Him. And even though we are to seek "a better country, that is, a heavenly one" (Heb. 11:16), we are not called to dismiss the place where God currently has us.

Before He was betrayed and given up to die, Jesus interceded in prayer to the Father for His disciples:

> 14 "I have given them your word, and the world has hated them because are not of the world, just as I am not of the world. 15 I do not ask that you take them out of the world, but that you keep them from the evil one." 16 They are not of the world, just as I am not of the world. 17 Sanctify them in the truth; your word is truth. 18 As you sent me into the world, so I have sent them into the world. 19 And for their sake I consecrate myself, that they also may be sanctified in truth.
>
> 20 "I do not ask for these only, but also for those who will believe in me through their word, 21 that they may all be one, just as you, Father, are in me, and I in you, that they also may be in us, so that the world may believe that you have sent me.
> **John 17:14-21**

As Christians, we are called to be distinct from the world even as we are "sent" (John 20:21) into the world. This is the tension we experience as missionaries.

In this prayer, what does Jesus reveal as our purpose in the world?

Jesus is clear that we will face trials. What role does the truth of God have in the lives of believers?

What does it look like practically to be in the world but not of it?

Though Esther was not a "missionary," she was placed by God into her position as queen (though she did not know for what purpose). Before Haman's plot was concocted, God had Esther in place. By risking her life and revealing her identity to the king, she was instrumental in saving God's people.

Though we may not find ourselves in such an extreme position, we still take hold of Jesus' promise:

> 32 Everyone who acknowledges me before men, I will also acknowledge before my Father who is in heaven,
> **Matthew 10:32**

Esther ultimately points to Jesus. Christ is the ultimate intercessor for His people. He prayed for your protection from the evil one and He now stands at the throne in heaven, identifying with you as part of His family.

You have nothing to fear. Jesus has put you where you are "for such a time as this" (Esth. 4:14) to continue His mission of taking His truth into the world so that others might believe and be saved.

PERSONAL STUDY 2

- -

PROVIDENCE AND RESPONSIBILITY

The Book of Esther holds together two truths in Scripture that can be challenging for us to fully comprehend.

1. **God's providence.**

2. **Human responsibility**

How have you wrestled with the tension between providence and responsibility? Why did you wrestle with understanding how one or both of those realities were true?

When has God's providence been an important truth with practical implications as to what you should do, not do, or how you should cope with a situation?

We see a healthy tension of both providence and responsibility expressed in Mordecai's question to Esther:

> Who knows whether you have not come to the kingdom for such a time as this?
> **Esther 4:14**

It is easy to discern the human responsibility side here. It is harder to discern God's providence, especially when God is not mentioned by name once in the entire book. But consider what scholar David M. Howard Jr. has to say on the matter:

"The best solution to God's absence from the book, however, would seem to be that the author is being intentionally vague about God's presence in events. Time and again the author seems to come close to mentioning God, only to veer away abruptly"[1]

We can perceive the vagueness of Mordecai's own words in both the question and his previous statement: "For if you keep silent at this time, relief and deliverance will rise for the Jews from another place" (Esth. 4:14). Mordecai did not believe in chance or fate. He was a Jew who worshiped a God who remained faithful to His covenant promises. So, why not just come out and say it?

Howard continues:

"By doing this, the author seems to be affirming, on the one hand, that God indeed is involved with His people (providence) and, on the other hand, that perceiving this involvement is sometimes difficult (God's hiddenness). While the author and his readers know (rationally) that God is always present and in control, the experiences of life show that the specific manifestations of His presence are not always so clear"[2]

Without a clear calling from God as received by Adam, Abraham, Moses, and Joshua, Esther determined her course of action by evaluating her position and the need of the people. In essence, she was embodying God's promise and purpose in the Abrahamic covenant (Gen. 12:1-3) — she was blessed (with the title of queen) so that she might be a blessing (to her people in peril).

What positions of influence has God placed you in?

What needs are around you that you may be able to help meet?

How has God seemed silent in areas of your life—maybe even the opportunities to meet needs and influence a situation for good?

The "hiddenness" of God also emphasizes the importance of prayer. Consider the request Esther made of Mordecai before she approached the king:

> [16] "Go gather all the Jews to be found in Susa, and hold a fast on my behalf, and do not eat or drink for three days, night or day. I and my young women will also fast as you do. Then I will go to the king, though it is against the law; and if I perish, I perish."
> **Esther 4:16**

Fasting would have certainly involved prayer (another veering off by the author of Esther). It is interesting that this is the first mention of fasting (and by extension, prayer) in the Book of Esther. It comes in response to the realization that she was (providentially) led to this position within the kingdom "for such a time as this." It comes in response to realizing that God had been with her and would use her. He was with her and would use her to do something extraordinary.

When was the last time you had the sense that God had uniquely positioned you to bring about some change?

What was the involvement of prayer (or even fasting) as you processed through your engagement in the situation?

Perhaps for the first time, you are hearing God speak directly to you through Mordecai's question: "who knows whether you have not come to the kingdom for such a time as this?" (Esth. 4:14).

We can risk losing whatever position we hold for the sake of others because, unlike Mordecai, we do not have to speculate where "relief and deliverance" will come. We know it has already come through Jesus Christ, who freely gave up His heavenly palace (Phil. 2:6-11) and perished to save us. We are free to risk for His kingdom because we know our future is secure in Him. All we have to do is acknowledge our opportunity.

TIPS FOR LEADING A GROUP

PRAYERFULLY PREPARE

Leading a group is a great responsibility and an incredible opportunity to let God use you in the lives of others. As you prepare for each session, always begin and end with prayer. Taking time to prepare for each session is critical for your group to grow and discuss God's Word. Take time before each session and prepare by:

Starting early. As you begin preparing to lead your group, make sure to start preparing in advance. If you meet weekly, don't wait until the day before. Instead, carve out time to look over each session a few days before so that you have the chance to allow God to speak to your heart.

Reviewing. Make sure to spend some time reviewing the last session you led.

Praying. As you pray for your group, consider the following:

Pray for each student by name. Not only pray that your group grows, but also spend time praying over the needs, requests, and hearts of each student. God has given you the opportunity to invest in the lives of students, and the way that He speaks to each one of us is just as unique as we are. As you pray for each member of your group, keep in mind how each one of them is growing and pray for God to walk with them in the midst of their joys and trials.

Pray for your group meeting. Ask the Holy Spirit to work through you and the group discussion as you point to Jesus in each session through God's Word. Your role is to help guide and facilitate discussion. Asking the right questions and guiding students to discover God's truth is more effective that simply telling students the right answer. Pray for the Holy Spirit's guidance as you lead.

Keep a prayer journal. Throughout the six sessions of this study, God will begin working in the hearts of each of your group members. One of the most powerful things you can do is keep a prayer journal to chronicle the many prayer requests, growth moments, and extraordinary breakthroughs students have. At the end of six sessions, you will have chronicled the spiritual journey of each one of your students so that you can look back as group and see how God has worked through this study.

INTENTIONALLY ENGAGE

Everything communicates something, and from the moment students arrive, you are setting the tone for your group. Creating a good environment starts when the first student arrives and ends when the final student leaves.

As students arrive for each session, focus on engaging each one of them.

> Remember to talk with each student as they come into your group meeting. The time before the session begins allows you a great opportunity to invest and simply catch up with students and get to know them better. This also allows you to meet new guests so they feel welcomed and cared for from the moment they come in.

> Don't allow anyone to feel excluded or alone. Interact with and include every student. Your group provides an opportunity for students to be in community with one another.

MINIMIZE DISTRACTIONS

Create a comfortable environment. If group members are uncomfortable, they'll be distracted and therefore not engaged in the group experience. Plan ahead by taking into consideration the following.

Seating. Ensure that all students have a place to sit so that everyone can connect and discuss with one another.

Temperature. Make sure the environment is comfortable for students to sit and engage in discussion without being distracted.

Food and drink. Providing food and drink is another way to help your students feel relaxed and create an enjoyable environment.

Surrounding noise. Find a quiet place where everyone can hear one another as they talk. Nothing is more difficult than trying to have a meaningful conversation in a noisy or public place.

General cleanliness. At best, thoughtfulness and hospitality show students and group members they're welcome and valued in whatever environment you choose to gather. The most important thing is that students are not distracted by the environment and surroundings. Do everything within your ability to help students focus on what's most important: connecting with God, with the Bible, and with one another.

Encourage discussion. A good small-group experience has the following characteristics:

Everyone participates. Encourage everyone to ask questions, share responses, and try to give each student an opportunity to read aloud.

No one dominates, not even the leader. Be sure that your time speaking as a leader takes up less than half of your time together as a group. Politely guide discussion if anyone dominates. Consider going around in a circle to respond or take turns reading Scripture. This method will help allow everyone to have a chance to speak without discouraging anyone from participating.

No one is rushed through questions. Don't feel that a moment of silence is a bad thing. Students often need time to think about their responses or to gain courage to share what God is stirring in their hearts.

Affirm students' input and responses by following up. Try to point out something true or helpful in each response. Don't just move on. Build community with follow-up questions, asking how other people have experienced similar things or how a truth has shaped their understanding of God and the Scripture you're studying. People are less likely to speak up if they fear you don't actually want to hear their answers or if they think you're only looking for a certain answer.

God and His Word are central. Opinions and experiences can be helpful, but God has given us the truth. Trust Scripture to be the authority and God's Spirit to work in students' lives. You can't change anyone—only God can. Continually point people to the Word and to active steps of faith.

Include others. Your goal is to foster a community in which students are welcomed just as they are. As you strive to include others, remember to encourage those involved to grow spiritually. Always be aware of opportunities to:

> › **Invite** new people to join your group;
> › **Include** any people who visit the group.

A somewhat inexpensive way to make first-time guests feel welcome or to invite someone new to get involved is to give them their own copy of this Bible study.

KEEP CONNECTING

Think of ways to connect with students during the week. Participation during the group session is always improved when students spend time connecting with one another outside the group sessions. The more comfortable and involved students are in one another's lives, the more they'll look forward to being together. When those in your group move beyond being acquaintances to truly being friends who form a community, they will be more likely to engage and particpate in the group.

Encourage group members with prayer, verses, and personal affirmation between sessions by using the following:

> **Email, text, social media and handwritten notes**

When possible, build deeper friendships by planning or spontaneously inviting group members to join you outside your regularly scheduled group time for:

> **Meals, fun activities, and projects around your church.**

GROUP INFORMATION

> **NAME:** _____

CONTACT INFO: _____

> **NAME:** _____

CONTACT INFO: _____

> **NAME:** _____

CONTACT INFO: _____

> **NAME:** _____

CONTACT INFO: _____

> **NAME:** _____

CONTACT INFO: _____

> **NAME:** _____

CONTACT INFO: _____

> **NAME:** _____

CONTACT INFO: _____

> **NAME:** _____

CONTACT INFO: _____

> **NAME:** _____

CONTACT INFO: _____

› **NAME:** _____

    CONTACT INFO: _____

› **NAME:** _____

    CONTACT INFO: _____

› **NAME:** _____

    CONTACT INFO: _____

› **NAME:** _____

    CONTACT INFO: _____

› **NAME:** _____

    CONTACT INFO: _____

› **NAME:** _____

    CONTACT INFO: _____

› **NAME:** _____

    CONTACT INFO: _____

› **NAME:** _____

    CONTACT INFO: _____

› **NAME:** _____

    CONTACT INFO: _____

› **NAME:** _____

    CONTACT INFO: _____

SOURCES

SESSION 2

1. Sandra Richter, *The Epic of Eden*, (Downers Grove, IL: Intervarsity Press, 2008), 158.

SESSION 3

1. Timothy R. Ashley, *The Book of Numbers* (Grand Rapids: Wm. B. Eerdmans Publishing, 1993), 210.
2. Timothy Keller, *Counterfeit Gods: The Empty Promises of Money, Sex, and Power, and the Only Hope that Matters* (New York, Penguin Books, 2009), xi.
3. Keller, xviii.
4. Darrin Patrick, *Church Planter: The Man, the Message, the Mission* (Wheaton, IL: Crossway Books, 2010), 164.
5. Patrick, 164.
6. Patrick, 165.

SESSION 5

1. Tremper Longman, III, *How to Read the Psalms*, (Westmont, IL: Intervarsity Press, 2009), 26.
2. Ibid.
3. Tim Keller, *Walking with God through Pain and Suffering* (New York: Penguin Books, 2013), 30.

SESSION 6

1. David M. Howard Jr., *An Introduction to the Old Testament Historical Books* (Chicago: Moody Publishers, 1993), 375.
2. Ibid.